# Preventive Care and Home Remedies for Your Computer

# The Healthy PC

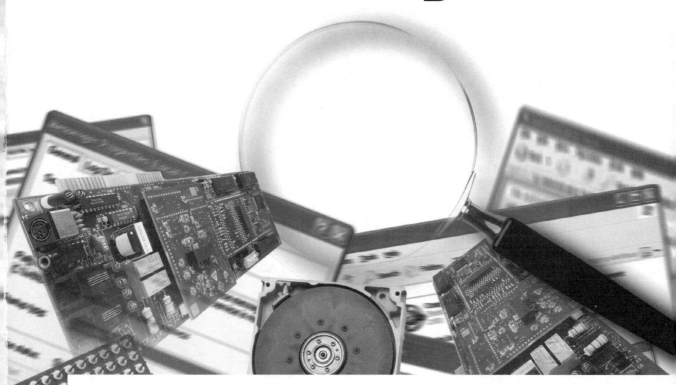

**Carey Holzman**

**McGraw-Hill** Osborne

New York   Chicago   San Francisco   Lisbon
London   Madrid   Mexico City   Milan   New Delhi
San Juan   Seoul   Singapore   Sydney   Toronto

The McGraw·Hill Companies

**McGraw-Hill**/Osborne
2100 Powell Street, 10th Floor
Emeryville, California 94608
U.S.A.

To arrange bulk purchase discounts for sales promotions, premiums, or fund-raisers, please contact **McGraw-Hill**/Osborne at the above address. For information on translations or book distributors outside the U.S.A., please see the International Contact Information page immediately following the index of this book.

**The Healthy PC: Preventive Care and Home Remedies for Your Computer**

4567890 FGR FGR 01987654

ISBN 0-07-222923-3

| | |
|---|---|
| **Publisher** | Brandon A. Nordin |
| **Vice President &** | |
| **Associate Publisher** | Scott Rogers |
| **Acquisitions Editor** | Margie McAneny |
| **Project Editor** | Carolyn Welch |
| **Acquisitions Coordinator** | Jessica Wilson |
| **Technical Editor** | Rob Shimonski |
| **Copy Editor** | Marilyn Smith |
| **Proofreader** | Susie Elkind |
| **Indexer** | Claire Splan |
| **Composition** | Tara A. Davis, Carie Abrew |
| **Illustrators** | Kathleen Fay Edwards, Melinda Moore Lytle, Michael Mueller |
| **Cover Design** | Pattie Lee |

This book was composed with Corel VENTURA™ Publisher.

## Dedication

This book is dedicated to my sister, Linda Rouse, who just a few years ago knew nothing about computers and today can fix most computer problems with her eyes closed. Her recent accomplishments are a great inspiration to anyone intimidated by computers. You can do it, too, and purchasing this book is a great first step.

# About the Author

**Carey Holzman** has over 13 years of professional PC repair experience and has been working with computers as a hobby since the early 1980s. He hosts his own weekly Internet-based radio talk show and frequently does PC-related presentations for local PC user groups.

For over seven years, Carey has owned his own company, Discount Computer Repair, in Glendale, Arizona, where he does computer repair, upgrades, and custom computer designs. He also does network and telephone wiring. Carey has worked at many major corporations including Intel, APS (Arizona's largest power company), SRP (Arizona's second largest power company), and the Arizona Department of Environmental Quality.

Carey was A+ certified in 1995 and has numerous other certifications from other computer-related corporations such as Hewlett-Packard and IBM. Carey has been featured in numerous computer and trade magazines across the world, including the *Toronto Star* in Canada and *Silicon Chip Magazine* in Australia, not to mention the *Glendale Star*, a local paper in Carey's home town. Carey also contributed to *The Home Networking Survival Guide,* a book by David Strom (published by McGraw-Hill/Osborne).

Carey also offers free advice and support at http://www.webpronews.com/careyholzman.html. And his web page with numerous PC tips and industry scandal news can be found at www.careyholzman.com.

# About the Technical Editor

**Robert J. Shimonski** holds over 30 technical certifications, including the CompTIA A+ and HTI+. He is a Microsoft Certified Systems Engineer on multiple platforms, including Windows NT and 2000, and is also a Lead Network Engineer for the Danaher Corporation. Robert worked his way up through the ranks, starting as a PC technician repairing and updating PCs. He has been building and maintaining PCs and teaching A+ classes in the New York area for years and loves to tweak PCs for maximum performance and security. Robert has worked on and published over 25 books and is the sole author of *Windows 2000 and Windows Server 2003: Clustering and Load Balancing,* published by McGraw-Hill/Osborne. You can contact Robert anytime at www.rsnetworks.net.

# Contents

vi    The Healthy PC

# Acknowledgments

This project started in February of 2003 and was in the works until October, 2003. During this time, I was graced to have such a talented crew from McGraw-Hill/ Osborne to direct me and help keep everything on track. I have to give extra special thanks to Francis "Franny" Kelly of McGraw-Hill/Osborne, and to Robert J. Shimonski, the book's technical reviewer. Without these fantastic people, this opportunity would never have existed.

I also want to thank the entire McGraw-Hill/Osborne crew: Tana Allen, Bettina Faltermeier, Margie McAneny, Marilyn Smith, Laura Stone, Carolyn Welch, Lyssa Wald, Lisa Wolters-Broder, and Jessica Wilson for all of the time and effort they invested into this project. Thanks also go to Nick Goetz for his work as developmental editor.

I mustn't forget to say thank you to my friends who helped me conquer some of the obstacles during the writing process—Michelle DePorter, Maralina Dvorak, Kyla Kahn, Ron Hillier, Steve Froehlich, Marc Abramowitz, Gerald Rosenbluth, Dana Pretzer, and Robert Beaubien. Thanks also go to my wonderful "guinea pig" test readers Stanley Skirvin and Ben Swank.

Of course, I have to give very special thanks and appreciation to my entire family for their continued support and encouragement during this project. This includes my dog Jake, who never left my side and never let me forget to take a break and go outside once in a while.

Finally, a huge thanks goes to my fiancé, Michelle Roiland, for her patience, understanding, support, and unconditional love. I love you, Michelle.

# Introduction

If you're like most people, you own a computer. And if you're like most people, you use it daily for work, play, and/or communication. But, like most people, when the computer crashes, (and it will crash at the moment you need it most), you have no idea what to do. Perhaps you read a book or two about computers supposedly designed for "dummies" or "idiots," only to discover that the topics and explanations were still very difficult to grasp. Perhaps someone in the family is a self-proclaimed "guru," or a colleague at work volunteered to help, and now the situation is even worse. Perhaps when you asked two different people for help, you got two different answers, and you don't know who to believe. So, you end up paying for a repair, knowing it had to be something simple that you could have fixed yourself, if only you knew a little bit more about computers.

If this sounds familiar, you've picked up the right book. Throughout the chapters in this book, I intend to show you how to:

- Perform preventive maintenance on your PC, along with virus removal

- Prevent spam (unsolicited junk email)

- Prevent Internet pop-ups

- Locate and remove all of the spyware (hidden programs that monitor your Internet activity) on your computer that you never knew were there

- Optimize your computer performance and your Internet connection speed

- Protect yourself against hackers

- Make a backup copy of your important files

- Upgrade your computer

- Maintain your computer hardware

- Solve common Windows problems

Notice that I said I am going to *show* you. I believe people learn better by doing, rather than by reading about doing. So, for each topic, you'll find simple instructions to follow each step of the way. Rather than talk all about how things work, I'll show you. That way, you'll get a better understanding of how things work—without the long, boring explanations. Treat this book as you would a cookbook. Each chapter contains simple and easy-to-follow step-by-step instructions presented just like a recipe.

Since most home computers are running a consumer version of Microsoft Windows, and since this book is aimed at the average home user, it will focus on Windows 98 (including Windows 98 Second Edition), Windows Millennium Edition (Me), and Windows XP Home and Professional. If you have Windows 95 or 2000, don't feel left out, because most of the information here still applies to your computer, although the steps offered won't match completely.

# Navigational Instructions

To follow the steps for keeping your PC healthy, you'll need to know how to interpret the instructions of this book.

## Using the Mouse

Throughout this book, there are numerous references to clicking, double-clicking, and right-clicking the mouse. All mice sold with or for Windows-compatible PCs have at least two buttons, and you use them as follows:

■ *Click* means to press and release, one time, the leftmost mouse button.

■ *Double-click* means to press and release twice, in quick succession, the leftmost mouse button.

■ *Right-click* means to press and release, one time, the rightmost mouse button.

NOTE *Throughout this book, you will be instructed to close windows when we are finished working in them. One easy way to close any window is to click the X in the top-right corner of the window.*

Items listed in **bold** throughout this book represent the exact wording and punctuation of what you should be looking for on your screen. It differentiates the Windows components you'll be instructed to use from the text of the book.

# Working on the Desktop

The *desktop* is the entire screen area that contains your wallpaper and icons, as shown in Figure 1. When you start a program, like Microsoft Word, it runs on top of your desktop, in many cases hiding your wallpaper and icons.

As you follow the instructions throughout this book, no programs should be running except for the ones you are instructed to run. Please close any running programs before starting any of the examples in this book.

Some people are uncertain if they've shut down all the running programs. For example, we're not concerned about antivirus software, which should *never* be turned off. We're concerned only with programs that have a button on the Taskbar. The Taskbar is typically at the bottom of your desktop and is usually gray or green in color. The Taskbar contains the famous Start button on its left side and has a clock

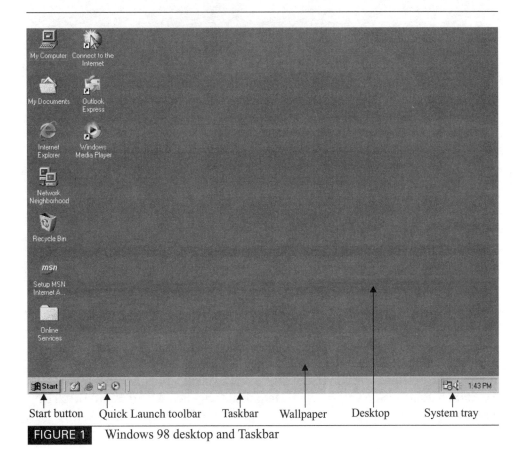

Start button    Quick Launch toolbar    Taskbar    Wallpaper    Desktop    System tray

**FIGURE 1**    Windows 98 desktop and Taskbar

on the right side. In between, little buttons appear for every program you run, as in this example:

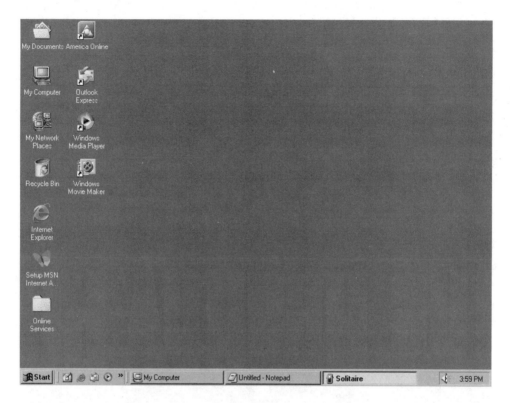

You want to make sure that the Taskbar does not contain any of these program buttons. No buttons means no running programs, and that's what you want before following the instructions in this book.

## Your Windows Version

This book covers the four current consumer-based Windows operating systems: Windows 98, Windows 98 Second Edition (SE), Windows Millennium (Me), and Windows XP (Home and Professional versions). You will find specific instructions to follow depending on which operating system you are running.

If you do not know which version of Windows you are using, simply right-click the **Start** button, click **Explore**, click **Help**, and then click **About Windows**. The window that opens will tell you all about your copy of Windows. Once you've determined which version of Windows you have, you can click **OK**, and then close the remaining window.

# All About Image

You might want to take this opportunity to configure your computer so that you'll be seeing everything exactly as demonstrated in the examples throughout this book. This setup is optional and affects only how things look on your computer monitor. It's up to you to decide if you wish to implement any or all of these suggestions. If you do follow the instructions here, the examples in this book will match what you see on your screen (regardless of which operating system you are running), and you shouldn't have any trouble finding icons or menu items that are referred to in this book. If you are a computer novice, then these steps are highly recommended.

## Putting My Computer on the Desktop

There will be references to the My Computer icon quite often in this book. If you are running Windows XP and do not have the My Computer icon located on your desktop, you can usually find it by clicking the Start button (unless your Start menu has been modified). If you would like to place the My Computer icon on your desktop for easier access (highly recommended), follow these easy steps:

1. Right-click any empty part of your desktop (not on an icon or in a window).
2. Click the **Properties** option.
3. Click the tab labeled **Desktop**.
4. Click the button labeled **Customize Desktop....**
5. Place a check in the box next to **My Computer**.
6. Click **OK**.
7. Click **OK** once more.

## Adjusting the Control Panel

Along with My Computer, you'll also be accessing the Control Panel quite frequently. You may find that your Control Panel does not look exactly like the examples in this book, particularly if you use Windows XP or Windows Me.

**NOTE**    *Windows 98 and 98 SE users can follow the directions offered for Windows 98. Windows XP Home Edition and Windows XP Professional Edition users should follow the directions offered for Windows XP.*

## Windows XP

To set up the Control Panel in Windows XP to look like Figure 2, follow these steps:

1. Click **Start**, and then click **Control Panel.**

2. If the top of your Control Panel says **Pick a category**, click **Switch to Classic View** (located on the left side of the window).

3. Click **View**, and then click **Icons.**

4. Click **View** again.

5. Click **Arrange Icons by**, and then click **Name.**

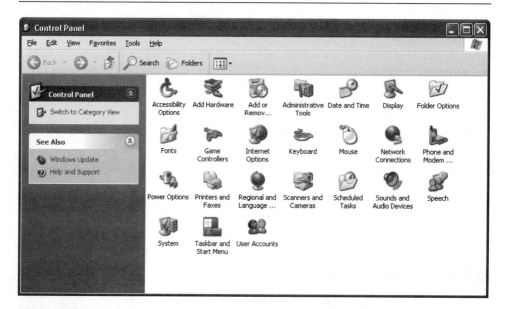

**FIGURE 2**    Windows XP Control Panel

Additionally, some Windows XP users may access their Control Panel by first clicking **Start**, and then clicking **Settings**. You can place the Control Panel directly on the Start menu for faster and easier access, by following these steps.

1. Click **Start**, click **Settings**, and then click **Control Panel**.

2. Double-click the **Taskbar and Start Menu** icon.

3. Click the **Start Menu** tab.

4. Ensure that the **Start menu** (*not* Classic Start menu) option is selected as shown in Figure 3, and click the **Customize** button.

5. Click the **Advanced** tab.

6. In the **Control Panel** options section, select **Display as link,** as shown in Figure 4, and then click **OK**.

7. Click **OK,** and then close the Control Panel.

**FIGURE 3**    Windows XP Start menu options

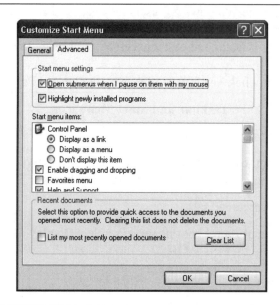

**FIGURE 4**    Windows XP Advanced Start menu options

## Windows Me

To set up the Control Panel in Windows Me, follow these steps:

1. Click **Start**, click **Settings**, and then click **Control Panel**.

2. On the left side of the Control Panel window, if you see **View all Control Panel options**, click it. The left side of the window should now offer to **Display only commonly used Control Panel options**.

3. Click **View**, and then click **Large Icons**.

4. Click **View** again.

5. Click **Arrange Icons**, and then click **by Name**.

## Windows 98

To set up the Control Panel in Windows 98, follow these steps:

1. Click Start, click **Settings**, and then click **Control Panel**.

2. Click **View**, and then click **Large Icons**.

3. Click **View** again.

4. Click **Arrange Icons**, and then click **by Name**.

## Adjusting the Display of Files and Folders

You can also adjust how Windows displays files and folders. Choosing a layout that is alphabetized and easy to read will help you to navigate and locate files, folders, and icons. Also, it's possible that double-clicking is disabled on your computer. Since many of the instructions in this book call for double-clicking, you should make sure that it's enabled.

### Windows XP

To set up your folder display and enable double-clicking in Windows XP, follow these steps:

1. Double-click **My Computer**.

2. Click **Tools** (in the menu bar across the top of the window).

3. Click **Folder Options…**.

4. Ensure **Show common tasks in folders** is selected.

5. Ensure **Open each folder in the same window** is selected.

6. Make sure the last option, **Double-click to open an item (single-click to select),** is selected. You should have the three options shown in Figure 5 selected.

7. Click **OK**, and then close the window.

### Windows Me

To set up your folder display and enable double-clicking in Windows Me, follow these steps:

1. Double-click **My Computer**.

2. Click **Tools** (in the menu bar across the top of the window).

3. Click **Folder Options…**.

**FIGURE 5**    If you are running Windows XP, make sure your screen matches
this picture.

4. Ensure **Use Windows classic desktop** is selected.

5. Ensure **Enable Web content in folders** is selected.

6. Ensure **Open each folder in the same window** is selected.

7. Make sure the last option, **Double-click to open an item (single-click to select)**, is selected. You should have the four options shown in Figure 6 selected.

8. Click **OK**, and then close the window.

## Windows 98

To set up your folder display and enable double-clicking in Windows 98, follow these steps:

1. Double-click **My Computer**.

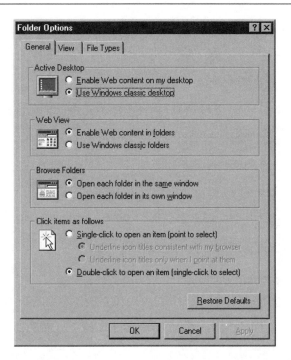

**FIGURE 6**    If you are running Windows Me, make sure your screen matches this picture.

**2.** Click **View** (in the menu bar across the top of the window).

**3.** Click **Folder Options…**.

**4.** Click the **Settings…** button (in the lower-right corner).

**5.** Ensure **Use Windows classic desktop** is selected.

**6.** Ensure **Open each folder in the same window** is selected.

**7.** Ensure **For all folders with HTML content** is selected.

**8.** Make sure that the last option, **Double-click to open an item (single-click to select)**, is selected. You should have the four options shown in Figure 7 selected.

**9.** Click **OK**.

**10.** Click **Close**, and then close the window.

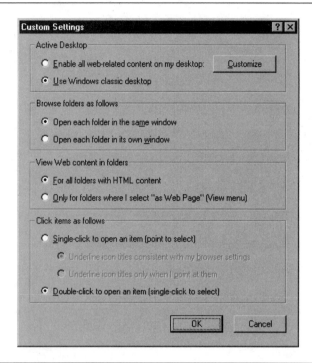

**FIGURE 7** If you are running Windows 98, make sure your screen matches this picture.

# Let's Get Started

One of the most frustrating aspects of being a computer technician is listening to all of the false information that is spread from person to person. Don't get me wrong—these people have the right intentions, but ultimately they are not helping anyone. Then, when customers ask me if what they have been told is true and I tell them no, they don't know who to believe. What you hold in your hands is a book that will teach you the right things, dispel the myths and hoaxes, and hopefully be entertaining along the way.

So, turn the page and get started turning your PC into a lean, mean, clean, efficient, and reliable machine! I promise, you can do it! When you're finished with this book, you're going to be the local guru.

# Part I

## Basic Maintenance

# Chapter 1

## Temporary Files, Internet Cache, Scandisk

Think of this book as you would a cookbook. Do not skip sections or pages and follow each step of the instructions offered. Explanations to terminology are offered just once as they are first introduced to you throughout this book. Also, certain tasks must be completed before starting subsequent tasks. If you haven't yet read the introduction to this book, I strongly recommend that you do so before going any further. There are optional instructions offered in the introduction for setting up your computer so that your screen will match the examples shown in this book (which may be helpful for following along). Much like a recipe, when you have completed the required steps, you will reap the rewards of your efforts, while learning at the same time.

This chapter will introduce you to "temp" files, as well as general hard disk check-up, cleanup and maintenance. If these words are foreign to you, don't worry. It will all be explained in great detail and useful analogies throughout each topic.

# Deleting the Temp Files

As you use your computer, files are moved, created, and deleted. They also shrink and grow in size. This includes files that Windows creates in order to operate properly. Some of these files fall under the category of Windows *temp files* (temp is short for temporary).

The problem with Windows temp files is that Windows quite often forgets about them. Windows is supposed to automatically remove the Windows temp files it creates, but in many cases, it does not. Over time, these files can take up quite a bit of hard disk space, not to mention adding unnecessary clutter. As a result, you may notice your computer performance will start to diminish as more and more hard disk space is needlessly consumed.

So, the first thing we are going to do is erase those Windows temp files and free that precious hard disk space. Have no fear, the Windows temp files contain nothing you need or will miss, so feel free to wipe them out them with impunity.

NOTE    *The part of your computer where all of your programs and data are stored is called your hard disk drive (HDD or hard disk for short). Most people have just one, and you may know it better as your C: drive.*

We are also going to use this opportunity to empty the Recycle Bin. As you delete files, they go into the Recycle Bin. Depending on the size of your hard disk, your Recycle Bin can potentially hold quite a bit of unneeded data. Just like a garbage can, it needs to be emptied from time to time.

Another part of this cleanup will be to delete all of the temporary Internet files. Temporary Internet files accumulate as you use the Internet (you'll learn more about this in Part II of this book).

The good news is Windows has a built-in, automated process to help you complete these tasks. The bad news is that Windows still tends to forget to remove many of the files. To keep things simple for now, we're going to start with this automated process and later, in Chapter 11, you'll learn how to do a much more thorough removal of *all* Windows temp files manually.

## For All Versions of Windows

1. Double-click **My Computer**.

2. Right-click on your **C:** drive. The menu that appears is called a shortcut menu.

3. Click **Properties** to open the Properties dialog box.

4. In the Properties dialog box, click the button labeled **Disk Cleanup**.

5. Place checks in each box to remove the following (not all of the items on this list may appear, depending upon which version of Windows you are using). Other options that may appear on your screen, but are not mentioned here (such as **Downloaded Program Files** shown in Figure 1-1), should remain unchecked or use your own discretion. If in doubt, leave it unchecked.

   ■ **Temporary Internet Files**

   ■ **Recycle Bin**

   ■ **Temporary Files**

   ■ **Temporary PC Health Files**

   ■ **Offline Web Pages**

   ■ **Application debugging information**

   ■ **Debug Dump Files**

   ■ **Old Chkdsk Files**

   ■ **Setup Log Files**

   ■ **WebClient/Publisher Temporary Files**

6. Click **OK** to execute the clean up.

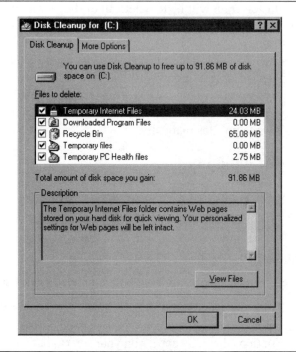

**FIGURE 1-1** Windows ME Disk Cleanup dialog

**7.** Click **Yes** when asked if you are sure.

**8.** When the task is finished, click **OK** to close the window, and then close the My Computer window.

## Enabling Automatic Cleanup in Windows XP

Windows XP has a built-in feature that can perform the disk cleanup operation for you at automated intervals, so you don't need to do it manually. If you would like to activate this feature, follow these steps:

**1.** Click **Start,** and then **Control Panel**.

**2.** Double-click **Scheduled Tasks**.

**3.** Double-click **Add Scheduled Task.**

**4.** Click **Next.**

5. In the alphabetized list that appears, click **Disk Cleanup,** and then click **Next.**

6. Choose how often you would like this task to run, and then click **Next.**

7. Select the time and day you would like this cleanup task to start, and then click **Next.**

8. If your computer is configured to ask for a password before allowing access to Windows, enter it here, and then click **Next**.

9. The applet, also called a *Wizard*, will inform you that your setup of this task was successful, and will show the name of the task and verify when it is scheduled to run. Click **Finish** and close the Scheduled Tasks window.

# Checking Your Disk with Scandisk

Scandisk has been included with every version of Windows since Windows 95. When you lose power or reset your computer improperly, you might recognize Scandisk as the application that runs after Windows scolds you that it has not been shut down correctly.

The purpose of the Scandisk utility is, literally, to scan your disk for logical and physical errors. A *logical error* is one where data is misplaced or corrupted. A *physical error* is one where the hard disk itself is damaged to some degree. Scandisk will scan floppy disks, Zip disks and, of course, hard disks. The larger your disks, the greater the opportunity for logical errors to occur within it.

For now, we'll select to do a quick, logical check with Scandisk. If you want to check your disk for physical errors at some point in the future, you can repeat the steps here and select the **Thorough** option under Windows 98/ME or its Windows XP equivalent, called **Scan for and attempt recovery of bad sectors**. This option can take a long time to complete. It is highly recommended that you run a Thorough test at least once; then you need to run it again only if you are experiencing problems with your PC.

## Running Scandisk with Windows 98/ME

Follow these steps to run Scandisk with either Windows 98 or Windows ME:

1. Double-click **My Computer**.

2. Right-click your **C:** drive and click **Properties**.

3. Click the tab labeled **Tools**.

4. Click the button labeled **Check Now**.

5. Select **Standard** as the type of test.

6. Place a check in the box next to **Automatically fix errors**.

7. Click **Start**.

Windows 98/Me users may experience the Scandisk utility starting over and never completing. If Scandisk has not completed within 10 minutes or you receive a message stating Scandisk has restarted ten times, asking if you want to continue, select **Cancel**.

This happens because another program (or programs) is running in the background and writing to the hard disk. This changes the contents of the disk, albeit slightly, but that's enough to make Scandisk need to restart. Think of it like this: Scandisk is counting continuously, 1, 2, 3, 4..., and some other program is shouting, "17!, 66!, 22!, 7!" Poor Scandisk must start all over.

It's important that nothing else is running on the computer when Scandisk is running. If a screensaver comes on, or if you start clicking icons or using programs, Scandisk may never be able to complete its check of the hard disk. See Chapter 9 for details on customizing your screensaver settings. (Windows XP users don't need to worry about this, because the XP version of Scandisk does not run within Windows.)

Some Windows 98/Me users may find that they need to boot into Safe Mode in order to get Scandisk to run properly. Safe Mode starts Windows in its most basic mode and is typically used when diagnosing a computer problem. Only the critical components necessary for Windows to function are loaded. For more information on Safe Mode, see Chapter 12.

As an alternative, there is a great free program you can download from the Internet called EndItAll, which should allow you to run Scandisk without the necessity of restarting the computer in Safe Mode. See Appendix F of this book for more information about obtaining this program, as well as other free software.

## Running Scandisk with Windows XP

Follow these steps to run Scandisk with Windows XP.

1. Double-click **My Computer**.

2. Right-click your **C:** drive and click **Properties**.

3. Click the tab labeled **Tools**.

4. Click the button labeled **Check Now**.

5. Select **Automatically fix file system errors**.

6. Click **Start**.

7. You must restart the computer for Scandisk to check the hard disk. Click **Yes**, and then click **OK** to close the Local Disk (C:) Properties dialog box.

8. Close the My Computer window.

9. Restart your computer by clicking on the **Start** button, clicking **Turn Off Computer**, and clicking **Restart**.

## Reading the Scandisk Report

Windows 98/ME users will be greeted with an informative report containing the results of Scandisk. Figure 1-2 shows an example of the Scandisk results.

Windows XP users will need to pull this information up manually, as follows:

1. Click **Start**, and then click **Control Panel**.

2. Click **Administrative Tools**.

3. Double-click **Event Viewer**, and then double-click **Application**.

4. Under the heading **Source**, double-click **Winlogon**, as seen in Figure 1-3. If you see more than one instance of 'Winlogon' listed, determine which is

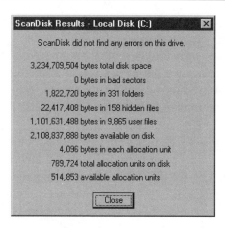

FIGURE 1-2    Windows 98/Me Scandisk results.

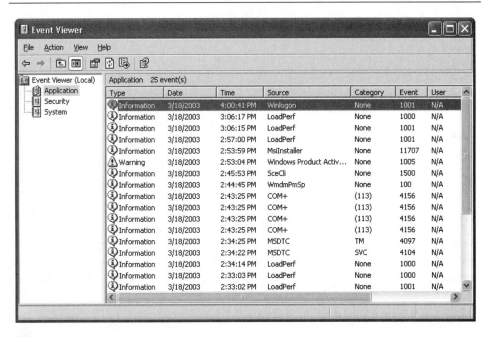

FIGURE 1-3   Event Viewer window in Windows XP

the most recent by looking at the date and time the report was created and select it. Figure 1-4 shows an example of the Scandisk results in Windows XP.

The only items we're interested in here are the total disk space, the space available, and whether or not there are any bad sectors. Windows assumes there are no bad sectors, unless it is specifically told to look for them (using the Thorough option described above). If bad sectors have been found in the past, it will remember and report them whenever Scandisk runs in the future. Typically, bad sectors are permanent and cannot be repaired. Windows XP Scandisk results may not make any mention of bad sectors if none exist.

If Scandisk finds bad sectors, that's an early indication of a failing hard disk. Although there is no certainty your hard disk will fail any time soon, bad sectors represent physical errors on the disk, and they will undoubtedly get worse as time goes by. Any data that happens to reside on a bad sector will be lost. Making a backup copy of your important data is highly recommended! Don't worry; we'll explain how to do that in Chapter 9.

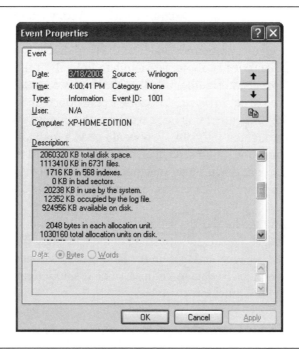

**FIGURE 1-4**    Windows XP Scandisk results

If the amount of available space is less than 10 percent of your total disk space, you should uninstall any unused software, as discussed in Chapter 8 of this book. If that doesn't free enough space, then it looks like you're in the market for a new hard disk, which we'll help you with in Chapter 10.

**NOTE**    *To help you determine what 10 percent of your disk space amounts to, you can use the calculator that's included with Windows. Simply click **Start**, then **Programs**, then **Accessories**, and then **Calculator**. Type in the large number that is reported as your "total disk space," then click the multiply button, type in the number 10, and click the percentage button.*

If there are any open windows on your desktop, now is a good time to close all of them.

# Defragmenting Your Disk

Defragmenting your hard disk is a free and painless way of increasing your data integrity and it may even help your computer run faster.

As data is erased or altered, or programs are removed, what remains are empty spaces throughout the hard disk where the data and/or programs used to reside. The next time data is saved or a program is added to the hard disk, it's placed in the first available space. If that space is not large enough to hold all of the data, it moves to the next available space, and so on, until all of the data is completely saved. This data is then considered to be *fragmented*, because it is no longer in one uninterrupted, or contiguous, piece. Imagine if this book were written that way. If the sentences were fragmented throughout the book, you would need a map to instruct you to go to a certain page, count down four sentences, read the third word from the left, then go to another page, count down seven sentences from the top, read the first word, and so on—until the entire sentence was reassembled. That's a lot of work and a lot of time.

By defragmenting the hard disk, you are reassembling all of the data back into contiguous pieces and, as a result, this leaves all of the remaining free space contiguous as well. This means less wear and tear on the hard disk, faster access to data, and less of a chance for a piece of data to get lost, since it's no longer scattered about.

To start the disk defragmenter:

1.  Double-click **My Computer**.

2.  Right-click on your **C:** drive and click on **Properties**.

3.  Click the tab labeled **Tools**.

    **For Windows 98/ME:**

4.  For Windows 98/ME, click the button labeled **Defragment Now**. For Windows XP, click the button labeled **Defragment**

Much like Scandisk, if the defragmenter is interrupted by other running software, it must start again from the beginning. Some Windows 98/ME users may need to run the defragment process in Safe Mode or use a utility such as EndItAll for the process to complete successfully, as with Scandisk (see "Running Scandisk with Windows 98/ME" section earlier in this chapter).

This process may take a long time, especially if you have a large or full hard disk and haven't done it in a long time (or ever!). Many people start to defragment their hard disk, power off their monitor, and then go to bed. By the time they wake up in the morning, the defragmentation process should be complete.

NOTE   *There are numerous third-party defragmentation programs available. While each one claims it's the most efficient, in my opinion, they are not necessary. The built-in Windows defragmentation software gets the job done well enough. While other programs might do a slightly better and/or faster job, they don't make enough of a difference to justify the added cost.*

# Summary

You've just learned how to safely remove unneeded files and free up precious hard disk space. You've learned how and why to Scandisk and defragment your data, and those words actually make sense to you!

I certainly don't recommend running these utilities every day. The hard disk must work very hard to defragment the data. This added wear and tear exceeds the normal wear and tear of everyday use and could cause your hard disk to fail prematurely. Generally speaking, for preventive maintenance, don't run Scandisk or the defragmenter more than once a week, but do run them at least once a month.

The Scandisk and Defragment utilities are generally considered to be preventive maintenance. You never *must* run them, but you should. Being alerted to bad sectors may be the only warning you receive before a hard disk fails. If you ever need professional data-recovery services, the technicians will have a better chance of recovering your data if the disk was recently defragmented prior to the failure.

Along with bad sectors, you won't believe what nastiness may lurk on your hard disk. In the next chapter, you'll learn how to identify and eliminate it, taking one more step in the direction of becoming a full-fledged computer guru!

# Chapter 2

# Improving PC Performance and Reliability

Many people discover that as time goes on, their PCs become more unstable and less responsive. In this chapter, you'll learn how to remedy the three most common causes of these symptoms by locating and eliminating viruses and spyware, along with learning how to locate and apply fixes and updates to your Windows operating system. By the time you finish this chapter, your PC should start up faster and run more reliably.

# Locating and Eliminating Software Spies

There are essentially four different kinds of software: retail software, freeware, shareware, and spyware. (In this book, I use the term *software* generically, to describe all computer programs.)

*Retail software* is just what its name implies: software you must purchase, either online or at a retail store.

*Freeware* is typically created by hobbyist programmers. They enjoy programming and offer their creations to others for free, with no strings attached.

*Shareware* is typically a program that is partially or fully functional for a limited period of time. The idea is that you get the opportunity to try the software out first before committing to purchasing it. Making the software only partially functional, or disabling the software after a certain period of time, motivates you to purchase the product if you find it useful. (See Appendix F for a list of some of the most useful freeware and shareware available, with brief descriptions and instructions on how to get the software.)

*Spyware* (sometimes called Ad-ware) is the newest form of software. Here, we'll take a look at what it is and what we want to do with it.

## What Is Spyware?

We currently live in an unusual economic climate. Software companies will pay programmers to write programs, promote those programs, host huge Internet sites, and give the software away for *free*. How can they afford to do that? With a little twisted marketing logic, it's easy. These companies include hidden programs within their freely offered program. These hidden programs, called *spyware*, monitor your Internet activity. They use your computer and your Internet connection to send information about the web pages you have visited, as well as your shopping preferences, back to the software company at regular intervals. The companies can then sell this information to other companies. The other companies can use that information to determine what kinds of items you might be interested in purchasing, based on the web sites you visited and items you have purchased in the past. In short, spyware is advertising-supported software. In addition, spyware can change your Internet startup page and alter important system files.

Of course, the companies that create this software don't think they're doing anything wrong. After all, the user (that's you) agreed to the terms and conditions prior to downloading and installing the software. These terms and conditions are typically presented in an *End User License Agreement* (*EULA*), and you must acknowledge that you read and understood this agreement before you are allowed to download or install the software. Most people never read the EULA. Those who do read it usually have no idea what any of the legal mumbo jumbo actually means.

Windows XP has a 28-page EULA that, in part, reads, "You specifically agree not to export or re-export the SOFTWARE PRODUCT (or portions thereof): (i) to any country subject to a U.S. embargo or trade restriction; (ii) to any person or entity who you know or have reason to know will utilize the SOFTWARE PRODUCT (or portions thereof) in the design, development or production of nuclear, chemical or biological weapons…"

As if anyone who would actually do this sort of thing would say, "Oh, I'm not allowed to do this? I guess I can't install the software. My plans are thwarted again! Darn you, Microsoft!"

But hidden within the legal mumbo jumbo of a spyware company's EULA is your agreement to allow the company to place tracking software on your computer, in exchange for some free software. You are also agreeing to let that software report back to the company regularly at your expense (it's using your computer and your Internet connection). You are also agreeing to not hold the company responsible if their software should cause any harm to your computer or data. Because you agreed to the terms and conditions prior to downloading and installing the software, this is considered legal.

## What's the Problem with a Little Advertising?

Not all advertising supported by software is bad. Some software can actually be quite useful and be worth the tradeoff. However, a big problem is that many programs that contain spyware cannot be uninstalled or do not completely uninstall, leaving the tracking pieces behind. As you continue to download and install free software, the spyware starts to accumulate on your PC. Instead of just having one or two programs spying on you, it's quite common to find more than 100! This typically results in your computer taking longer to start up (also called *booting*), poor computer performance overall, reduced resources available to other programs (see Appendix C to learn more about resources), as well as system lockups and crashes, not to mention taking up valuable space on your hard disk.

To make matters worse, some of these spyware companies attempt to trick you into downloading their spyware-laced software by displaying fake Windows error messages that appear quite genuine. These fake messages may say things like:

```
Your Computer is Currently Broadcasting an Internet IP Address
Your Internet Connection Is Not Optimized
Your Current Connection May Be Capable of Faster Speeds
```

Figure 2-1 shows some examples of these fake messages. Once you click the OK button, you are whisked away to the spyware company's web site.

> **NOTE** *Windows is considered to be a graphical user interface, also known as a GUI (pronounced "gooey"). It uses pictures (graphics) to communicate (interface) with you (the user). A new term was coined to refer to the fake error messages produced by Internet advertising companies. They are known as a fake user interface, or FUI (pronounced "fooey").*

What might concern you the most about spyware is that you have no way of knowing or controlling what information is being sent out from your computer. Sure, the spyware companies claim they are not collecting any sensitive or identifiable data, but how do you know that for a fact? The only way to know for sure is to remove any and all traces of spyware from your computer!

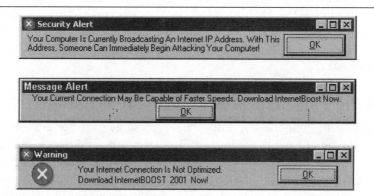

**FIGURE 2-1**    Some Internet advertising that uses deceptive fake user messages to trick people into visiting web sites

## How Can You Locate and Remove Spyware?

There are numerous freeware and shareware utilities designed to help rid you of spyware. Currently, there are two that stand out as better than the rest: Ad-aware, by Lavasoft, and Spybot Search & Destroy, by PepiMK Software. Download and install them to decide for yourself which one you like better, or better still, use them both.

NOTE   *You will need an Internet connection to acquire this software. If you do not have (and have never had) an Internet connection, then you will not have downloaded any of this free software or fallen victim to web sites that install spyware without your knowledge, and you can safely skip this section.*

Once you detect and remove the spyware, be warned that the program the spyware belonged to will usually stop working. At this point, you have two choices:

- Go back to the company's web site and re-download and reinstall the software, knowing it will place some spyware on your computer.

- Learn to live without that piece of software.

NOTE   *Web pages and software tend to change quite frequently over time. The instructions here are for the version of the web page and software that were currently available during the writing of this book. You should be aware that your screen may not match the examples offered here because some of the steps may have changed as the software is updated since the publication of this book. The procedures shouldn't change drastically as the software is improved over time, and those changes should only make the software easier to use.*

To acquire and use the two spyware-removal utilities previously mentioned, simply follow these easy steps:

### Using Ad-aware

Our first stop will be the Ad-aware web site. To download and install Ad-aware, follow these steps:

1. Click **Start**, and then click **Run.** In the window that appears, type **www.lavasoftusa.com.** Then click **OK**.

2. On the web page that appears, locate and click **Download**.

3.  Choose to download a copy of the current version of Ad-aware by clicking one of the Ad-aware links listed under **Full Install**.

    The Ad-aware software is stored in several locations throughout the Internet, and each link on the **downloads** page takes you to a different place where you can get the program. You can choose any one of the links to start your download. If the download does not start for any reason, try again using a different link.

4.  The next window that appears warns you that, "Some files can harm your computer. If the file information below looks suspicious, or you do not fully trust the source, do not open or save this file." Of course, we trust this source; after all, we selected it. If this window ever appears unexpectedly, I would recommend pressing the **Cancel** button. You are asked if you want to **Open** or **Save** the file you are about to download. I suggest that you click **Open**. When the download completes, the software will automatically start to install.

5.  When prompted, click **Next**. The EULA appears. As always, satisfy yourself that the EULA doesn't contain anything that you feel can cause you distress. Click **Next** to continue the installation.

6.  The destination folder (where the software will install itself) is displayed. Click **Next** here, and then click **Next** once more to begin the installation.

7.  When the installation completes, click **Finish**.

Now that you have Ad-aware installed on your computer, you can run it to remove any spyware you happen to have. Close any open windows, but keep your Internet connection on. Then follow these steps:

1.  Double-click the Ad-aware icon on your desktop.

2.  Before scanning your computer, check to see if any Ad-aware updates are available. Updates are extremely important because they instruct the software what to define as spyware. Because spyware is written and changed on an almost daily basis, the definitions change. Ad-awares' database must be updated prior to using it to recognize these latest forms of Spyware. On the screen, locate and click the option **Check for updates now**, and then click the **Connect** button. If an update is available, accept it by clicking **OK**. Once the update is complete, click **Finish**.

**3.** The Ad-aware software has its own **Start** button. Click that button to start the spyware-scanning process. Then choose **Use default scanning options** and click **Next**.

The scanning process may take awhile, depending on the speed of your computer and the size of your hard disk. Please be patient and allow it to complete. When it has finished scanning your hard disk for spyware, your computer will buzz (if you have speakers and they are turned on) and the top of the Ad-aware window will say Scan Complete, as shown in Figure 2-2.

**4.** Click **Next** to see what Ad-aware found. Each item in the list should have a check in the box next to it. You might want to take a moment to scroll through the list and see if any of these items look familiar. Although I recommend that you leave all the boxes checked, if there are any items you recognize and do not wish to remove, you may uncheck the box next to it. If the items listed are unchecked, you can easily place a check next to all of them by right-clicking your mouse over a selection and choosing "Select all objects."

**5.** Click **Next,** and when you are asked if you want to continue, click **OK**. All of the spyware will be deactivated and placed into a quarantine file on your hard disk, in case you want to reactivate any of it.

**6.** Close the Ad-aware program.

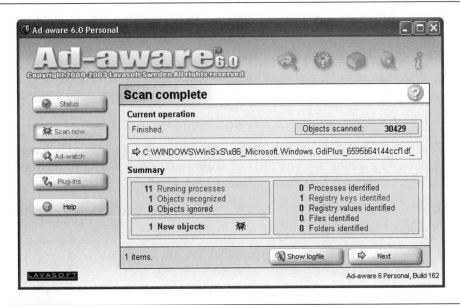

**FIGURE 2-2**   Ad-aware version 6.0 after its scan has completed

The Ad-aware program has some very useful and informative built-in help. You can access this information at any time by clicking the **Help** button.

## Using Spybot Search & Destroy

The other spyware-removal program you may want to download and run is Spybot Search & Destroy. To download and install this program, follow these steps:

1. Click **Start**, and then click **Run.** In the window that appears, type **http://spybot.safer-networking.de.** Then click **OK**.

2. On the web page that appears, locate and click **Download**.

3. Choose to download the current version of Spybot Search & Destroy by clicking one of the links offered. If one is available, choose a link that says "direct download."

   Like the Ad-aware software, the Spybot Search & Destroy software is stored in several locations throughout the Internet, which you can access through the download links on this web page. If the download does not start for any reason, try again using a different link. The links that are not labeled "direct download" offer other software as well. If a direct download link is not available, click another link and look through the list of available software to locate and select Spybot Search & Destroy.

4. You will be asked if you want to **Open** or **Save** the file you are about to download. I suggest that you click **Open**. When the download completes, the software will automatically start to install.

5. When prompted if you want to continue to install Spybot Search & Destroy, click **Yes**.

6. When the welcome screen appears, click **Next**.

7. The EULA is displayed. As always, satisfy yourself that the EULA doesn't contain anything that you feel can cause you distress. Select **I accept the agreement** and click **Next** to continue the installation.

8. The destination folder of where the software will install itself is displayed. Click **Next,** and then click **Install** to begin the installation.

9. When the installation completes, click **Finish.**

Now you're ready to run Spybot Search & Destroy. Close any open windows, but keep your Internet connection on. Then follow these steps:

1.  Double-click the Spybot Search & Destroy icon on your desktop.

2.  Select the language in which you would like the program to be displayed.

3.  A warning message explains that some programs that require spyware will no longer run once you remove the spyware portion. Click **OK**.

4.  Updates are extremely important because they instruct the software what to define as spyware. Because spyware is written and changed on an almost daily basis, the definitions change. The Spybot Search & Destroy database must be updated prior to using it to recognize these latest forms of Spyware. The next screen reminds you to check for program updates before scanning. Click **OK**.

5.  The next screen simply asks if you would like to remove the Spybot Search & Destroy icon from your desktop, or if you would like to have Spybot Search & Destroy start automatically when your computer starts. These choices are entirely up to you. After you've chosen how you want the program to behave, click **Next.**

6.  Click **Search for updates,** and then click **Download all available updates** if it is offered. If there are updates, the software will apply them and then restart itself.

7.  Once you are at the main program screen, click **File,** and then click **Check for problems**.

8.  When the check is complete, Spybot Search & Destroy will show a list of the spyware items it found, as shown in Figure 2-3. Each item in the list should have a check in the box next to it. You might want to take a moment to scroll through the list and see if any of these items look familiar. Although I recommend that you leave all the boxes checked, if there are any items you recognize and do not wish to remove, you may uncheck the box next to it.

9.  Click **Fix selected problems** to eliminate all of the recognized spyware from your hard disk.

10.  Close the Spybot Search & Destroy program.

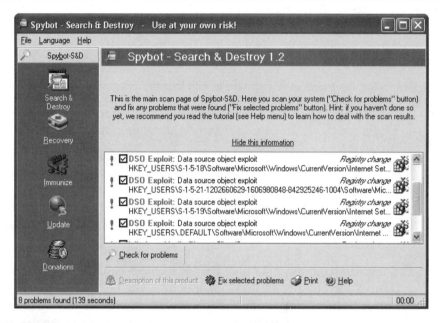

**FIGURE 2-3**  Spybot Search & Destroy version 1.2 after it has completed scanning a hard disk

The Spybot Search & Destroy program has some very useful and informative built-in help. You can access this information at any time by clicking the **Help** option at the top of the window.

# Antivirus: Does This Look Infected to You?

You've probably already heard a lot about viruses and the potential harm they can cause. The stories can be downright scary. It's important to remember that a computer virus is nothing like a human virus. A computer virus is just a program that runs on your computer, like any other software. If you're properly prepared, you can detect and remove many viruses fairly quickly and painlessly.

## What Can a Virus Do?

A *virus* is a program designed to automatically migrate to other computers, and it can do so without any user interaction. Most viruses also carry a *payload*, which is a separate set of instructions, typically designed to cause some kind of harm, such as:

■ Format your hard disk, which will result in the destruction of all data and programs on the hard disk.

■ Place random messages on your screen, just to be annoying.

■ Delete random files from your hard disk.

■ Send random files from your hard disk to random people in your address book, by using your e-mail program, without your knowledge.

■ Send itself to everyone in your address book, by using your e-mail program without your knowledge.

These are only a few examples of the potential harm a virus can cause. Not all viruses have payloads. Some viruses do nothing at all.

In April 1994, there were 3,000 known viruses. In May 1996, that figure grew to 9,000. Today, there are more than 58,000 catalogued viruses, with 10 to 15 new viruses discovered each and every day. To have a computer without antivirus software installed is not just risky—it's practically a guarantee that your computer will be (or currently is) infected. It's imperative that you update your antivirus software constantly in an effort to keep yourself protected from the most recent viruses.

## How Does Antivirus Software Work?

In order for antivirus software to work effectively, it must be told how to recognize a particular virus. Consider how many post offices across the United States contain posters with pictures of the FBI's "most-wanted" criminals. The idea here is that if you recognize the person in the photo, you'll contact the FBI. If the posters were never updated, the information would become obsolete over time. In much the same way, antivirus software must be kept up-to-date with the equivalent of digital fingerprints of the most recently discovered viruses, while at the same time still remembering all the viruses of the past.

Since viruses never die or become extinct, the list can only grow larger. If your antivirus hasn't been updated recently (or ever!), your computer could be infected even now!

There are also Trojans and worms, which many people consider to be in the same category as a virus. A *Trojan* is a program that appears useful, but inside lurks a nasty virus just waiting to be released. Remember the story of the Trojan horse? That's the source of this nasty software's name.

A *worm* is a program that is designed to replicate itself in as many places as possible: all over your hard disk, through your e-mail, across networks, on the

Internet, and even on floppy disks. Worms never take a break, and they work extremely fast. They can tie up networks and cause crashes. Have you ever tried to call a radio station to win a contest? Were you ever able to get through? So many people dialing at once creates a never-ending busy signal. This is the equivalent of what a worm can do to a network, or even to the entire Internet.

## What Kinds of Viruses Are There?

Different kinds of viruses have different kinds of effects on your computer. These are the main types of viruses currently being distributed:

- *Boot virus*    This kind of virus infects the very beginning of the hard disk. It's the first thing the computer sees when you turn it on, even before the Windows screen appears. Boot viruses can be some of the most difficult viruses to remove.

- *File infector virus*    This kind of virus attaches itself to certain types of files across your hard disk. When you run that file, it activates the virus.

- *Macro virus*    This kind of virus attacks only applications—like Microsoft Word, Excel, PowerPoint, Access, Lotus AmiPro, and so on. It is typically harmless, causing problems that are usually just annoying and frustrating. The virus activates only when the application it's associated with is in use.

- *W32 virus*    This kind of virus infects Windows programs such as Notepad, Solitaire (gasp!), and even your screensaver.

- *Script virus*    This kind of virus is often transferred by e-mail and is actually embedded into the e-mail itself (like a tick on a dog). Sometimes, just opening the e-mail to read it can cause your machine to become infected.

- *Multipartite virus*    This type of virus is a combination, typically, of a boot virus and a file infector virus. You get two for the price of one!

- *Mutation or polymorphic virus*    This kind of virus can be any of the viruses mentioned above, but it also attempts to elude detection by changing its structure. Every time the virus starts, one of the first things it does is change its "fingerprint." Think of it as the chameleon of viruses.

Reading about all of these different types of viruses may make you nervous. But don't worry; with current antivirus software, you can protect yourself from *all* viruses.

## Darwinism: Why Do Viruses Exist and Who Creates Them?

Why we have viruses is a difficult question to answer. Why do some people spray-paint graffiti or make prank phone calls? Many viruses are written by young computer adventurers, testing and expressing their programming skills and their curiosity to see what can happen. Some do it to gain knowledge, some for fame, and some to prove themselves worthy to join underground virus gangs. Others may write viruses because they seek attention, revenge, or the challenge to defeat antivirus software. Other virus creators may be bored, vandals, or sociopaths. The possibilities are endless.

Some virus writers don't create viruses from scratch. In many cases, they'll take an existing virus and add or change a small part of it, thereby creating a new virus, resulting in a twisted sort of virus evolution.

Some conspiracy theorists speculate that the antivirus software makers also write some of the viruses. That certainly would help boost the sale and dependency of antivirus software. However, there has never been any evidence that this has occurred.

NOTE    *Virus creators are not considered to be hackers. Hackers are people who enjoy pushing software to its limit in an effort to see what it's capable of, learning every detail about the software, with no intent to cause any harm. They may be considered much like racecar drivers with their cars. They are generally considered to be good guys.*

## Self-Defense: How Can I Protect Myself?

Here are some general guidelines that will help you to avoid getting a virus:

- Install antivirus software and keep it updated.

- Since most viruses are spread through e-mail, don't accept files or programs from people you don't know.

- Never activate any file that arrives in e-mail, even if it is from someone you know, *unless* you have up-to-date antivirus software running at all times.

- When uncertain about a file sent by e-mail, assume it's a virus.

- Only download files that are from a legitimate and respectable source.

- When starting your computer, make sure there are no floppy disks inserted into the floppy disk drive.

- Keep your Windows operating system updated with the latest security fixes (discussed in detail next).

- Make sure your computer is free of viruses before you back up your data; otherwise, you may be backing up the virus, too! (Making backup copies of any important files on your computer is the best thing you can do to protect yourself, as discussed in Chapter 9.)

The two most successful and reliable antivirus programs are McAfee VirusScan and Norton AntiVirus. Figure 2-4 shows an example of a Norton AntiVirus window. While there are literally dozens of antivirus programs available, these are the two that detect the largest number of viruses consistently. Not all antivirus software is created equal.

If you simply cannot afford to buy either the McAfee or Norton program, you can download a fully functional copy of AVG antivirus for free from www.grisoft.com. It may not be as refined or as reliable as the commercial programs, but something is better than nothing. (For more information about AVG antivirus, see Appendix F.)

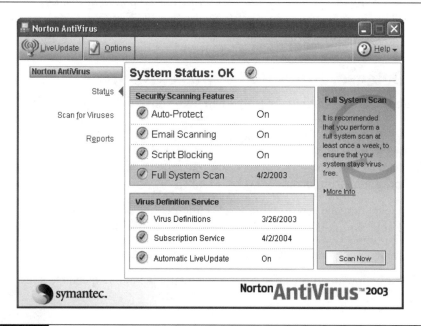

**FIGURE 2-4**    A Norton AntiVirus software window

# This Old Windows

When programmers write software, they must be careful to watch for loopholes (or *bugs*) in their code that could cause the program to not behave as it should (or *crash*).

If I were to leave out a very important chapter of this book, that would be considered an oversight. In computer language, we call that a *bug*.

## A Bug's Story

The most famous bug to date was known as the Y2K bug. This bug wasn't actually a programming mistake, but an oversight by bureaucratic managers who failed to properly follow up on decisions they made years before.

Initially, when computers were first used in businesses, memory and hard disk space were at a premium. The programmers were instructed to save as much space as possible by writing software as efficiently as they could. One way to save space was to assume that the first two digits of any year entered into the computer would always be *19*. Because computers were new and technology was evolving quickly, it was assumed this software would be replaced or updated long before the year 2000. However, because the software continued to meet the company's needs year after year, few were willing to spend the money to fix something that wasn't broken. Once companies were reminded of the way in which the software was written many years ago, most of them had no idea whether or not this bug would affect them without first doing research.

Your phone bill is an example of how important the date can be. When you make a long-distance call or use a cellular phone, you are billed for the length of time that call lasted. A computer does this automatically. It's programmed to record the exact date and time that you initiated the call and when you terminated the call. It's then programmed to subtract the start time from the end time to determine how many minutes you used. In relation to the Y2K bug, consider what would happen if you placed a phone call before midnight in 1999 and didn't end that call until after midnight of the year 2000. If the program were instructed to use only the last two digits of the year, it would derive a negative number (subtracting 99 from 00 results in –99!). The software wasn't designed to work with negative numbers, and things would start failing as a result. The billing system couldn't create bills, because the information it was provided would be invalid, which means the printers couldn't print the invoices, and so on.

If the software were to stop functioning, we would call this a *crash*. In some cases, a crash is caused by a bug, but there are other reasons for crashes. (Be grateful this terminology exists only with computers. Imagine if your car would crash when you hit a bug!)

Sometimes, programmers write a piece of software designed to fix another piece of software. We call that an *update* or a *patch*. Software is usually given a version number, so you can tell whether your software has all the patches. The alternative to patching the software would be to completely uninstall the program, obtain the complete and latest version of that program, and then completely reinstall it.

NOTE *As programs become easier to use, they require more programming code, which results in more internal complexity. That results in more opportunity for bugs and unrecognized interactions to exist and for crashes to occur. In fact, attempted fixes for bugs sometimes introduce new bugs!*

Since Windows 98, Microsoft developed a unique way to keep Windows up-to-date by introducing the Windows Update web site. Theoretically, if your software is kept up-to-date, your computer will run and work better.

## What Kinds of Updates Are There?

Microsoft offers a number of different types of updates. All of these are available through its Windows Update web site:

- *Critical updates and service packs*   These are typically patches designed to keep your computer stable and secure. They are considered to be critical to the operation of your computer. When several individual updates are combined into a single package, it is referred to as a *service pack*.

- *Recommended downloads*   These are typically enhancements designed to increase ease of use and versatility of Windows and many programs that work with Windows.

- *Windows tools*   These are typically utilities and other software tools designed to enhance performance and facilitate upgrades.

- *Internet and multimedia updates*   Just as the name implies, the latest versions of Internet Explorer and Windows Media Player are offered here, when they are available.

■ *Additional Windows downloads*    These are updates for your desktop settings and other Windows features.

■ *Multi-language features*    These updates implement the use of other languages in your Windows menus and dialog boxes.

■ *Driver updates*    A *driver* is a specific piece of software that tells a specific version of Windows how to communicate with a specific piece of hardware. Your modem, printer, video card, and sound card all require their own specific drivers to work properly within Windows. An inefficient driver can affect the performance and reliability of Windows, so it's important to install the latest drivers available to ensure your computer is running optimally.

## How Do I Stay Current?

You can visit the Windows Update web site to see what updates are available, read about what they do, and choose which ones you would like to get. Then you can download and install your selected updates.

To use the Windows Update web site, follow these steps:

1. Click **Start**, and click **Run.** In the window that appears, type **www.windowsupdate.com**, and then click **OK**. (Alternatively, you can choose the Windows Update option in your Start menu.)

   If this is your first visit to the Microsoft Windows Update web site, or if you haven't been there in quite some time, a message will appear, similar to one shown in Figure 2-5. Microsoft is asking you for permission to install a small Internet program (called an *ActiveX control*) that can analyze your computer to determine which operating system you have, what hardware you are using, and which updates you are missing.

2. Click the **Scan for updates** link. A progress indicator will keep you informed of the status of the scan. Once it completes, if you require any updates, it will show those on the left side of the window, grouped into categories, as shown in Figure 2-6.

3. Any critical updates your computer is missing will be selected automatically. To acquire them, click **Review and install updates,** and then click the **Install Now** button.

   Be aware that some updates may need to be installed before other updates can be installed. If more than one critical update is available, it's quite

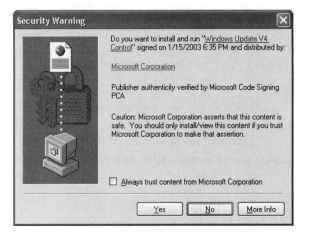

FIGURE 2-5 The dialog box that appears when you visit the Microsoft Windows
Update web site for the first time

FIGURE 2-6 Windows Update showing numerous available updates

possible you will receive a warning message, similar to one shown in Figure 2-7, stating that a specific update must be installed on its own first. Simply click **OK** if you receive this message, and the Windows Update site will automatically cancel the other updates.

**CAUTION**    *If you install critical updates, you will most likely be prompted to restart your computer after the download and install process. Make sure you have saved any work and quit all programs before choosing to restart the computer.*

**4.** After this update process has completed successfully, click **OK** when asked to restart your computer.

Once you have successfully applied all of the critical updates and restarted your computer, you may find that the Windows Update web site now shows some new critical updates for your computer. This happens when there is an update to an update. After you restart your computer—after installing an update from the Windows Update web site—be sure to return to the Windows Update web site. Keep checking until there are no more critical updates available.

## How Can I Find Out about New Critical Updates?

Critical updates are crucial to keeping your computer secure and as bug-free as possible. But how do you know when new critical updates become available?

Since the release of Windows 98, Microsoft included a utility within Windows that will periodically check to see if your computer is missing any available critical updates. This is the recommended way to keep your computer up-to-date from now on.

**NOTE**    *Ironically, Microsoft has even released an update to its critical update notification feature. You may have seen this while visiting the Windows Update web site.*

**FIGURE 2-7**    A message that appears when an update needs to be installed separately

To activate automatic notification of critical updates, follow the easy steps for your particular Windows system.

## For Windows 98

The Critical Update Notification feature for Windows 98 can only be enabled or disabled; no other options are available. To enable Critical Update Notification, just download it from the Windows Update web site.

After you have downloaded and installed Critical Update Notification, it will check for updates every five minutes when your computer is connected to the Internet, and it will alert you when new critical updates are available, as shown in Figure 2-8. (If you later want to disable Critical Update Notification, you must uninstall it using the Add/Remove Programs icon in the Control Panel.)

## For Windows ME

Windows ME improved on the Windows 98 Critical Update Notification system and changed its name to Automatic Updates. To reduce user intervention, when new critical updates become available, Windows ME will automatically download them. Microsoft also added more options for the user to customize. Here are the steps for using this feature:

1. Click **Start**, click **Settings**, and then click **Control Panel.**

2. Double-click **Automatic Updates**.

3. Select **Automatically download updates and notify me when they are ready to be installed.**

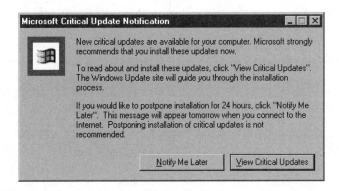

FIGURE 2-8   A Microsoft Critical Update Notification alert in Windows 98

4.  Click **OK** and close the Control Panel.

5.  After you have activated Automatic Updates for the first time, a small globe icon appears next to the clock on the right side of the Taskbar. Click this icon.

6.  You are prompted to read and accept the EULA. The Automatic Updates process will not start until you have accepted the EULA. If you choose to not accept the EULA, Automatic Updates will not work.

When Automatic Updates discovers an update is ready to be installed, a message will appear briefly above the clock on the right side of the Taskbar, and the small globe icon will reappear. When you click on this message or on the small globe icon, you'll see a dialog box, similar to the one shown in Figure 2-9, which contains the following three buttons:

■  **Settings**   This is where you can customize the Automatic Updates process. (This is the same screen that appears when you double-click on the Automatic Updates icon in the Control Panel.)

■  **Remind Me Later**   Think of this as a snooze button for the Automatic Updates process. You can specify that Windows remind you later, so that an update installation does not interfere with your current computer activity.

■  **Install**   Begins the installation process of the updates.

## For Windows XP

Windows XP offers the Automatic Updates feature through its System Properties dialog box. Follow these steps to turn it on:

1.  Click **Start**, click **Control Panel,** and then double-click **System**.

2.  Click the tab labeled **Automatic Updates.**

3.  Place a check in the box next to **Keep my computer up-to-date. With this setting enabled, Windows Update software may be automatically updated prior to applying any other updates.**

4.  Select the option **Download the updates automatically and notify me when they are ready to be installed.**

5.  Click **OK** and close the Control Panel.

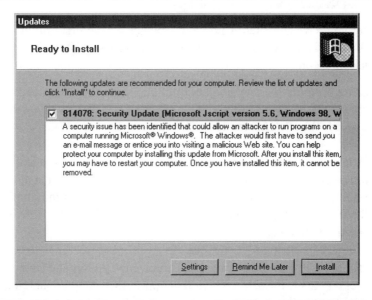

**FIGURE 2-9**    An Updates dialog box in Windows ME, which appears after you click the globe icon (shown in the lower-right corner) when new critical updates are available

After you've turned on this feature, when Automatic Updates discovers an update is ready to be installed, a message will appear briefly above the clock on the right side of the Taskbar, and a small globe icon will also appear. When you click on this message or on the small globe icon, you'll be offered the option to see details or to install the updates. If nothing happens when you click the globe icon, that means the update is still being retrieved from the Internet. Try again in a few minutes.

## Summary

In this chapter, you've learned what spyware is, why it exists, how you get it, how to locate it, and how to remove it. Then you learned how to keep nasty viruses off your system and why it's so important to be virus-free. You also discovered why software updates are so important and how to configure Windows to alert you as soon as new critical updates become available.

Now you can use the words *Trojan*, *worm*, *bug*, *crash*, *driver*, and *hacker* in sentences that you can actually understand. You also know what EULA, GUI, and FUI stand for. But wait, don't purchase that geeky propeller hat just yet. In the next chapter, you're going learn all about the Internet, starting with getting around on it faster!

# Chapter 3

## Optimizing Your
## Internet Connection

The Internet can be a wonderful and magical place, but for many of you, that place may seem distant. It's a lengthy trip from your computer to your favorite web site. In this chapter, I'll show you how to configure your Windows settings to use your Internet connection as efficiently as possible.

There are literally hundreds of software titles available that make grand claims about increasing your Internet speed. Ironically, you can even download software that claims to speed up the downloading of software. Some of these programs are free, and some are available for a charge. Unfortunately, few of these programs actually make any difference at all in your Internet speed.

Using high-octane gasoline in an economy car *may* result in a slight performance difference. Installing a larger engine, on the other hand, will definitely improve performance. Whether you connect to the Internet using your telephone line and a modem (economy car) or you have a high-speed DSL (Digital Subscriber Line), broadband cable, or satellite connection (race car), the tips in this chapter will ensure you're getting the most from it.

# For Dial-Up Modem Users Only

There are many different speeds of modems. Just as cars with larger engines have more power, modems with higher connection speeds will transfer data faster. Without going into too much detail, you most likely have a 14.4k, 28.8k, 33.6k, or 56k modem. (The *k* is short for thousand, or "000," and is borrowed from the metric measurement of kilo.) The smaller the number, the slower the modem. Since your Internet service provider (ISP) charges you the same price regardless of your modem speed, it makes sense to have the fastest modem possible.

## What Does 56k Actually Mean?

No 56k modem will ever connect literally at 56k. Any connection over 33.6k is considered a 56k speed because it requires a 56k-capable modem. In order for your modem to connect at 56k speeds, it must communicate with another modem using the same type of 56k technology that your modem supports. As explained in the previous section, there are currently four different 56k standards—X2, K56flex, V.90, and V.92—and three of them are incapable of communicating with one another at speeds higher than 33.6k.

## 56k Modem Incompatibilities Explained

When 56k modems were first introduced in 1996, there were two competing standards. One was called K56flex, introduced by Lucent Technologies and Rockwell Semiconductor. The other was called X2, developed by U.S. Robotics. The International Telecommunications Union (ITU), a standards committee, needed time to determine which one of these 56k technologies should be the standard. Because both technologies worked equally well, combined with the fact that there were millions of consumers who were eager to pay for faster modems, the companies felt they could not wait indefinitely for the ITU to decide on a standard. As a result, each company began selling and marketing its product to the public.

Because a 56k K56flex modem was incompatible with a 56k X2 modem, in order to achieve a 56k connection, your ISP needed to provide the same type of 56k implementation that your modem supported. This was very confusing for consumers, and often resulted with ISPs needing to provide multiple access numbers dedicated to supporting each technology. Many consumers purchased a 56k K56flex modem, only to find out that their ISP only supported X2, or vice versa.

It wasn't until almost two years later, in February 1998, that the ITU finally agreed on a universal standard to be used for 56k connections over telephone lines. They called it V.90. Now there were three different types of 56k modems! But wait, there's one more! Late in the year 2000, the ITU approved three enhancements to 56k and called this newest standard V.92.

## 56k Modem Facts

Just because you have a 56k modem doesn't necessarily mean you wouldn't benefit from replacing it. Here are some facts you should know about 56k modems:

- A 56k modem will connect no faster than 53k because it would exceed telephone line power consumption rules set forth by the Federal Communications Commission (FCC).

- A 56k speed may not be possible on everyone's telephone lines. Some older wiring that still exists may not be capable of carrying a 56k signal.

- A 56k connection using the K56flex, X2, or v.90 standard will affect your download speed only. When uploading, your data is still sent at the slower 33.6k speed. In other words, your computer can retrieve data almost twice as fast as it can send data.

### 56k V.92 Modem Facts

Here are some facts that pertain to 56k V.92 modems:

- When you upload data, it can go as fast as 48k. This means that you can send files at nearly twice the speed of the older V.90 standard.

- If you have call waiting provided by your telephone carrier, you can install modem-on-hold software (usually included with your new V.92 modem or available for download from your modem's manufacturer) that will notify you if there is an incoming call. This allows you to take the incoming call while placing your Internet connection on hold. When you're finished with your call, your computer is instantly back online.

- When your computer connects to another computer, that initial noise you might hear is called a *handshake*. The old K56flex, X2, and V.90 handshake lasts 25 to 30 seconds, which is the time it needs to test the line to see if it's capable of a 56k speed. The length of time the handshake requires with a V.92 modem has been reduced to about half.

- A V.92 modem will connect just fine to a V.90 modem, but the unique features of V.92 will not be available during that connection.

## How Can I Determine Which Modem I Have?

Through the Windows Control Panel, you can get information about your modem. The specific steps depend on which Windows version you have.

### Checking the Modem Type on Windows 98/ME Systems

To discover which modem you have installed on your Windows 98/ME computer, follow these steps:

1. Click **Start**, click **Settings**, and then click **Control Panel**.

2.  Double-click the icon labeled **Modems.** The brand and speed of your
    modem will be displayed in the dialog box, as shown in Figure 3-1.

    If you have a 56k modem and are now wondering if you have X2, K56flex,
    V.90, or V.92, continue as follows:

3.  Click the tab labeled **Diagnostics.**

4.  Click the COM port designated to the modem, as shown in Figure 3-2.

5.  Click the button labeled **More Info.**

6.  Your computer will query the modem, and then will display a screen full
    of responses from the modem. You will need to scroll through this list of
    "modem-speak," as shown in Figure 3-3, and look for the term *X2, K56flex,
    V.90,* or *V.92* to determine the type of 56k your modem supports.

7.  When you are finished, click **OK.**

8.  Click **OK** and close the Control Panel.

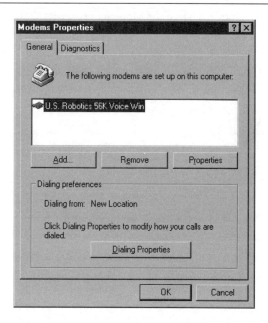

FIGURE 3-1    The General tab of the Modems Properties dialog box in Windows 98

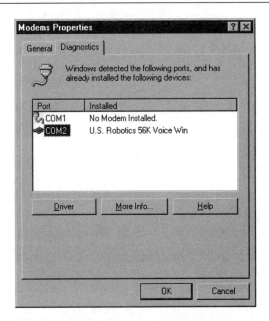

The Diagnostics tab of the Modems Properties dialog box in Windows 98

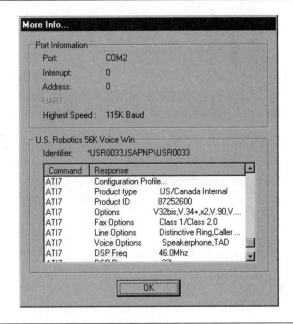

Scrolling down to nearly the bottom of the page shows that this modem supports "V32bis, V.34+, X2, V.90…"

## Checking the Modem Type on Windows XP Systems

To see which modem you have installed on your Windows XP computer, follow these steps:

1. Click **Start**, and then click **Control Panel**.

2. Double-click the icon labeled **Phone and Modem Options.**

3. Click the tab labeled **Modems.** The brand and speed of your modem will be displayed in the dialog box that appears similar to Figure 3-4.

   If you have a 56k modem and are now wondering if you have X2, K56flex, V.90, or V.92, continue as follows:

4. Click the button labeled **Properties.**

5. Click the **Diagnostics** tab, and then click the button labeled **Query Modem.**

6. Your computer will query the modem, and then will display a screen full of responses from the modem, similar to what is shown in Figure 3-5. You will need to scroll through this list of "modem-speak" and look for the term *X2, K56flex, V.90,* or *V.92* to determine the type of 56k your modem supports.

FIGURE 3-4    Phone and Modem Options screen from Windows XP

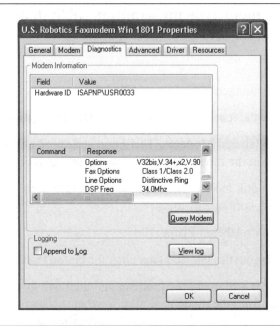

**FIGURE 3-5**  Modem properties page and Query response as seen in Windows XP

**7.** When you're finished, click **OK**.

**8.** Click **OK** and close the Control Panel.

## How Can I Get a Faster Connection?

If you do not currently own a 56k modem, or if your 56k modem is not V.90- or V.92-compliant, you should upgrade it. Because of the popularity of high-speed (also called broadband) Internet connections, the price of modems has come down tremendously. It's not uncommon to find new 56k V.92 modems available for less than $30.

In Chapter 10, you'll learn just how easy it can be to replace your modem. This will have a much greater impact on your Internet connection speed than any tune-up or software could ever provide.

Regardless of your modem speed, there are some settings you can change to take advantage of the best performance possible from your modem and computer. Again, the steps depend on which Windows system you have.

## Adjusting Modem Settings on Windows 98/ME Systems

To change modem settings on your Windows 98/ME computer, follow these steps:

1. Click **Start**, click **Settings**, and then click **Control Panel.**

2. Double-click the **Modems** icon.

3. Click the button labeled **Properties** located in the middle of the window (Do *not* click the Dialing Properties button located at the bottom of the window.)

4. Ensure that your **Maximum speed** is set to **115200.**

5. Click the tab labeled **Connection,** and then click the **Port Settings...** button.

6. Ensure **Use FIFO buffers (requires 16550 compatible UART)** has a check placed in the box next to it.

7. Windows 98 users, set your **Receiver Buffer** and your **Transmit Buffer** to **High** and click **OK.**  Windows ME users, set your **Receiver Buffer** and your **Transmit Buffer** to **Maximum** and click **OK.**

8. Click the **Advanced** button. The next dialog box that appears should look like the example in Figure 3-6.

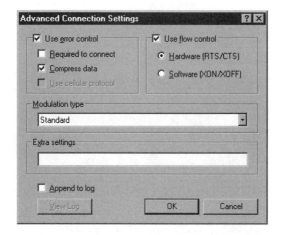

FIGURE 3-6    Recommended modem settings in Windows 98/ME

9.  Ensure a check is placed next to **Use error control**, no check is placed next to **Required to connect**, and a check is placed next to **Compress data.**

10. Ensure a check is placed next to **Use flow control** and that **Hardware (RTS/CTS)** is selected.

11. Make sure Modulation Type is set to **Standard.**

12. When you're finished, click **OK.**

13. Click **OK** and close the Control Panel.

## Adjusting Modem Settings on Windows XP Systems

To change modem settings on your Windows XP computer, follow these steps:

1.  Click **Start**, and then click **Control Panel.**

2.  Double-click the icon labeled **Phone and Modem Options.**

3.  Click the **Modems** tab and click the **Properties** button.

4.  Click the **Advanced** tab and click the **Advanced Port Settings…** button. The next dialog box that appears should look like the example in Figure 3-7.

5.  Ensure **Use FIFO buffers (requires 16550 compatible UART)** has a check placed in the box next to it.   √

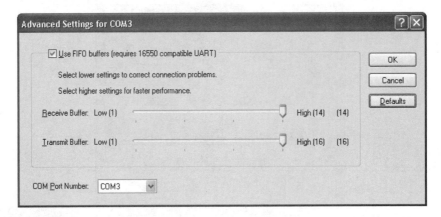

**FIGURE 3-7**    Recommended modem settings in Windows XP

6. Set your **Receive Buffer** and your **Transmit Buffer** to **High**.

7. When you're finished, click **OK**.

8. Click **OK** and close the Control Panel.

## How Fast Is My Modem Connecting?

Your modem can be instructed to report the communication speed between itself and your computer (DTE, for data terminal equipment) or the speed between itself and another modem (DCE, for data communication equipment). If your modem reports that you are connecting at 38,400, 57,600, or 115,200, it's reporting the DTE speed. You will need to refer to your modem documentation or contact your computer manufacturer's technical support to find out how to instruct the modem to report the DCE speed instead.

If you use America Online (AOL), the speed is reported immediately during the logon process. Alternatively, once you're at the main AOL Welcome screen, simply click **Help** (located at the top of the window), click **About America Online,** and then, while holding down the CTRL button on your keyboard with one finger, press the letter Y on your keyboard with another finger; then release both buttons. The window that appears should look similar to Figure 3-8. It contains your connection status information, including your current connection speed.

For all other Internet connections, you should see a graphic of two tiny computer screens next to the clock in your system tray, which is located on the right side of your Taskbar, as shown in Figure 3-9. If you double-click this icon, a window will appear showing your connected speed.

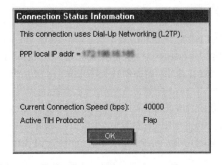

**FIGURE 3-8**   An AOL connection status window, showing a current connection speed of 40,000

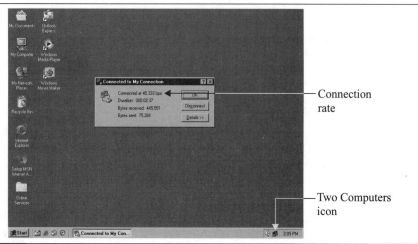

Connection rate

Two Computers icon

**FIGURE 3-9**    Dial-up connection information in Windows ME

**NOTE**    *It is quite common for your connection speed to vary each time you connect. How the call is routed by the telephone company will determine if your ride is a smooth one (high connection rate) or a bumpy one (low connection rate).*

If you have a 56k modem and the number you see is 36,000 or higher, you are connecting at a reasonable 56k speed. If your 56k modem connection speed is below 36,000, disconnect and redial. If your connection is consistently below 36,000, here are some other things you can check:

■ A broken or frayed telephone cord running from your computer to the wall can affect connection quality. Make sure it is a good, clean cord. If you are uncertain, replace it with a new one.

■ You can call your local telephone company and ask them to run a free line test on your telephone line. If they detect any noise on the line, it's their responsibility to fix it if the problem is located outside your home (unless you have the optional telephone line insurance, which will cover the cost, regardless of the source of the problem). Many times, after it rains, an exposed telephone wire will become wet, and your connection speed will suffer until it dries. This is the best time to call the telephone company and request a line test.

■ Most ISPs offer numerous local telephone numbers to connect to their service. Try different access numbers until you find one that works fastest for you.

■ Consider replacing your modem, especially if it's over two years old. Remember that just because it appears to be working, doesn't necessarily mean it's working correctly. You'll find details on how to pick the right modem and install it in Chapter 10.

■ Prevent the transmission of unnecessary information. Internet pop-ups, spam, viruses, advertisements, and spyware can clog your Internet pipeline. All of this is discussed in detail in Part II of this book.

**NOTE** *If your connection speed is good, but the Internet is still sluggish, it may just be the Internet. There are times, similar to rush hour on a freeway, when the Internet has more traffic. However, if it's always sluggish, complain to your ISP. Sometimes an ISP can have more customers than they have available bandwidth.*

# For Broadband Cable Modem, DSL Modem, and Satellite Users Only

Your Internet speed may seem fast, but there's a good chance your computer is not configured to use the full potential of your Internet connection. Fortunately, there are free services on the Internet that can analyze your computer configuration, test it, and then make recommendations.

## How Can I Check My Internet Connection Configuration?

You can tweak your Internet connection configuration as follows:

1. Click **Start**, and then click **Run**. In the window that appears, type **www.dslreports.com/tweaks** and click **OK**.

2. Toward the bottom of the page that appears, you'll see a small window labeled Tweak Tester II. Below this window, click the button labeled **Start** to begin the test.

3. When the test completes successfully, when instructed to do so, click the **Results** button.

4. The next screen that appears requires some information from you:

   ■ **Service**   This is a drop-down list in which your choices are displayed. If you are uncertain about what kind of service you have, contact your ISP's technical support.

■ **Speed** This is how fast your ISP says your connection is. It may be on a recent invoice, or you may have to contact their technical support to find out. Typical speeds are 128k, 256k, 640k, 1MB, 1.5MB, 2MB, or 3MB. If you have a 640k connection, type **640** in this window. If you have a 1MB connection, type **1000** in this window.

■ **Operating System** Choose the operating system you are currently using from the drop-down list.

■ **Connection** For most people, you will leave this at Normal. However, if you are unsure what kind of connection you have, contact the technical support department of your ISP.

Once you have answered these four items, click the **Recommend** button.

5. The screen that appears will be chock-full of information. Since most of this information is technical, the test makers help you by placing an icon below their Notes and Recommendations. You want to see little happy face icons under all of their Notes and Recommendations. If you have anything other then happy face icons, follow the steps to correct your computer configuration.

6. Once your configuration changes are complete, restart your computer and run the test again.

7. Repeat this process until only happy face icons appear under the Notes and Recommendations sections.

Now you know your computer is utilizing your Internet connection as efficiently as possible, and you didn't need to spend a penny!

As an alternative to this method, you may visit www.SpeedGuide.net and click the **TCP/IP Optimizer** link. When offered, choose to **Open** the program. Once your download completes, click the option for **Optimal settings** (found at the bottom of the window that will appear), and then click the **Apply changes** button. Your computer will need to be restarted for these changes to take effect. You can find numerous other Internet speed tips, tweaks, and enhancements on this web site. Try them at your own discretion.

## How Can I Determine My Internet Speed?

There are several web sites on the Internet that can measure the data-transfer speed of your Internet connection. Here are a few options for testing your Internet speed:

- Click **Start**, click **Run**, type **www.2wire.com**, and click the **Bandwidth Meter** link.

- Click **Start**, click **Run**, type **www.dslreports.com/stest**, and follow the on-screen directions.

- Click **Start**, click **Run**, type **http://computingcentral.msn.com/Internet/speedtest.asp**, and follow the on-screen directions.

NOTE

*There are a number of variables that can affect the speed that is reported, such as your distance from the testing web site and how busy the testing web site is. Run the speed test a few times over the course of a day and average the scores. The average speed should be close to what your ISP advertises.*

# Summary

In this chapter, you learned how to get the most for your money by optimizing your Internet connection, but there's still more work to be done. Computers have the ability to *multitask*, which means they can do many things at the same time. Your computer may be continuously sending and receiving information over the Internet without your knowledge or permission. Next, you'll learn how to put an end to those annoying pop-up ads, spam, other forms of Internet advertising and unwanted "visitors" that tie up your connection, your computer, and your patience.

# Part II

# Internet 101

# Chapter 4

# Internet Cookies, Temporary Internet Files, and Pop-ups

As if keeping your computer operating properly wasn't enough, advertisers on the Internet like to utilize it to do their bidding, too. They love it when your computer is fast, powerful, and responsive! They'll use as much of your computer and your Internet connection, which you unknowingly allow, hawking their wares and even attempting to scare you into purchasing their products. They may even be so bold as to advertise a product that gives you control over how to stop all advertisements! To make matters worse, they can typically make a perfectly functional computer very frustrating to use. Of course, once they've "warned" you about all the "dangers" of not having their product, it leaves you confused about whether what they said is true or not. Who do you believe? With all the recent talk of Internet cookies, temporary Internet files, and pop-ups, you must need to buy something to protect yourself, right? WRONG! This couldn't be further from the truth. Put away your wallet, because you're about to learn how to end all of this nonsense and take back control of your own computer.

# Internet Cookies

Cookies have received a lot of bad publicity and, as a result, many people want to know how to remove them from their computer. First, you need to understand that having Internet cookies on your computer is not necessarily a bad thing.

An Internet cookie is typically used to remember specific information about the last time you visited a particular web site. For example, when you visit a web site where you shop, it may place items you have selected to purchase into a virtual shopping cart. If you exit the web site without purchasing any of the items you placed in the shopping cart, it will remember the contents of your shopping cart the next time you visit.

Thanks to Internet cookies, you can specify your personal preferences of features that a web site may offer, such as to display the current weather conditions of the city you live in or to automatically enter your user name and password if one is required for that particular web site. Then, each time you visit that web site in the future, it automatically recalls your preferences. These types of cookies are called *first-party* cookies.

There are also *session* cookies, which are temporary cookies that exist only while you are currently visiting a web site. Once you leave that web site, the cookie is removed.

## How Do Internet Cookies Work?

When a web site remembers your preferences, it does so by saving that information on the *web site's* computer, and then assigns that information a unique identification tag. The web site places only the identification tag information on your computer, using a very small text file with a unique name. The next time you visit that web site, it checks to see if you have this text file on your computer, and if so, what identification tag it contains.

A common misconception is that an Internet cookie is a program that web sites place on your computer to collect data at will about your computer usage. An Internet cookie is not a program, and it cannot read any data from your hard disk, including the data stored in other cookies. Also, no other computer can read the cookie except the one that gave it to you. The only information a cookie will ever contain is information you specifically provided.

Simply put, an Internet cookie is a unique tag that is placed on your computer that essentially says, "You were here." It's a simple way you can identify yourself to web sites you visit. Any information associated with your identity is kept on the web site's computer.

## So What's All the Fuss About?

There are several clever, unscrupulous marketing companies that add cookies to their Internet advertisements. If you visit a web site that contains one of these advertisements, the *advertisement* places a cookie on your computer. These are referred to as *third-party* cookies.

Once you have a third-party cookie stored and happen to visit another site that uses the same marketing company, it will recognize the third-party cookie on your computer and be able to determine not only what page you were visiting when it recognized you, but also your computer's IP (Internet Protocol) address. The marketing companies won't know what you do with the pages you view, but from knowing what pages you visit and how often, they can target specific advertisements to appear on your screen that they think you will be interested in based on that information. This isn't the same as collecting personal information such as your e-mail address or tracking your every move when you are online.

 *The act of being on the Internet is commonly referred to as being online. Saying, "I am currently on the Internet" or "I am currently online" is the same thing.*

## Taming the Cookie Monster

As previously mentioned, Internet cookies aren't all bad. Using a spyware detection and removal utility, such as those discussed in Chapter 2, will help eliminate the bad cookies while leaving the good cookies alone.

## Why Are They Called Cookies?

While many rumors abound, it is commonly believed that the term *cookie* comes from a prank program called Cookie, which was invented at MIT around 1970. The program was based on the Cookie Monster character from the Children's Television Workshop television program "Sesame Street." The Cookie Monster was always on the lookout for more cookies, and he would quite often say to anyone, "Give me a cookie!"

When this Cookie software was activated on an unsuspecting person's computer, it would randomly interrupt whatever the person was doing with the demand, "Give me a cookie!" The person then had to type the word *cookie* to make the program go away (temporarily). If the user typed anything other than the word *cookie*, the software would just repeat itself and prevent the user from continuing work until its demand was met. So, from this practical joke program, *cookie* metaphorically came to mean something given on demand to a remote host.

The politically correct computer nerds do not like the term *cookie*. They believe a cookie is nothing more than a nondescriptive, meaningless, misplaced name for the more accurate computer term, *token*.

As you struggle to understand computers, keep in mind that many seemingly complicated terms, such as cookie, aren't really complicated at all. For example, before the World Wide Web, a *Gopher* server was a standard way for files and information to be made available on the Internet. It was called a Gopher because that was the mascot of the University of Minnesota, where it was invented. An archive searching software engine was named Archie, and improvements to it were named Jughead (Jonzy's Universal Gopher Hierarchy Excavation And Display) and Veronica (Very Easy Rodent-Oriented Net-wide Index to Computerized Archives). If you have a scanner attached to your computer, you most likely installed a TWAIN driver. TWAIN stands for Technology Without An Interesting Name. Those terms don't seem so serious and complicated anymore, do they?

### Blocking Third-Party Cookies

Since prevention is always the best medicine, you'll learn how to configure your computer to accept only first-party and session cookies, and to deny all third-party cookies. Follow these steps to block only third-party cookies:

1.  For Windows 98/Me, click **Start**, click **Settings**, and click **Control Panel**. For Windows XP, click **Start** and click **Control Panel**.

2.  Double-click the icon labeled **Internet Options**.

3. Click the **Privacy** tab and click the button labeled **Advanced**.

4. Place a check in the box next to **Override automatic cookie handling**.

5. Select **Allow** under **First-party Cookies**.

6. Select **Block** under **Third-party Cookies**.

7. Place a check in the box next to **Always allow session cookies**. Your screen should now look like Figure 4-1.

8. Click **OK,** click **OK,** and close the Control Panel.

## Deleting Cookies

If you want to, you can delete all Internet cookies from your computer. However, keep in mind that since an Internet cookie enters your name and password automatically to specific web sites that require such information, you will be required to enter your name and password manually on future visits to these web sites after you've erased all Internet cookies from your computer.

To erase all Internet cookies from your computer, follow these steps:

1. For Windows 98/Me, click **Start**, click **Settings**, and click **Control Panel**. For Windows XP, click **Start** and click **Control Panel**.

2. Double-click the icon labeled **Internet Options**.

3. The General page opens. Click the **Delete Cookies...** button, which is in the middle of the page, under **Temporary Internet files**, as shown in Figure 4-2.

**FIGURE 4-1**    How to block "bad" cookies but allow the "good" ones

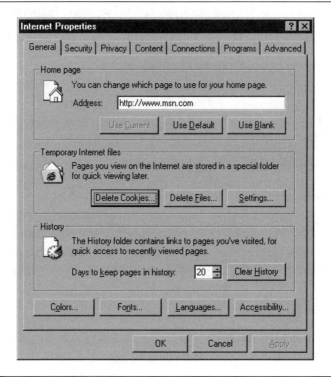

**FIGURE 4-2**  Using the Internet Properties dialog box to delete all Internet cookies

4. You will be asked if you wish to proceed or cancel this request. Click **OK** to proceed if you are sure you want to permanently delete all Internet cookies (good and bad) from your computer.

5. When the process is complete, click **OK**, and then close the Control Panel.

# Temporary Internet Files

When you visit a web site, all of the graphics (pictures) and text (information) that appear on your screen are saved to a dedicated area on your hard disk. The idea is that by saving these files to your hard disk, you will save time when you visit the same web site in the future, because your computer will not need to download the same information again.

NOTE *When you are sending information over the Internet, we call that uploading. When you are receiving information from the Internet, we call that downloading.*

## Downloading versus Installing

Some people confuse the term *downloading software* with *installing software*. *Downloading* describes a specific way in which someone can acquire the software by receiving it from the Internet. If you purchase the software at a store, you are not downloading it. Once you have the software, whether you downloaded it or purchased it at a store, you then install it. This terminology can make a big difference when your friend makes the statement, "I downloaded Windows on my computer."

Microsoft never made Windows available to download, so if your friend really did download Windows, he did it illegally. This is referred to as *pirating*, a word describing software theft. Perhaps what your friend really meant to say was that he *installed* Windows on his computer. See how using the proper terminology can make a difference?

This raises many privacy concerns for some people, because it effectively leaves a record of the web sites you have visited. Depending on how large the temporary Internet file area is on your hard disk, someone could theoretically look back through months, or even years, of your Internet history. By default, Internet Explorer sets aside three percent of your total hard disk space for temporary Internet files. For example, if you have an 80-gigabyte (GB) hard disk, Internet Explorer will reserve 2.4GB of it solely for your temporary Internet files. That is a lot of history and hard disk space.

## Are Temporary Internet Files Good or Bad?

Temporary Internet files are good, if you visit a web site regularly. Storing the entire contents of the web page on your hard disk can give you the impression that the page is loading faster on future visits because it simply grabs the information locally from your hard disk rather than globally over the Internet.

Temporary Internet files are bad, if you don't want to give other people who have access to a computer you are using the ability to discover where you have been. Perhaps you're afraid that if your boss discovers pictures, sounds, text, and/or movie clips from www.espn.com on your work computer, you could be reprimanded, or worse, lose your job. Most employers today record and review their employee's computer usage for simple liability reasons. However, there is rarely a need to purchase any software to methodically erase your Internet history. The only exception would be if you have a computer genius for a relative that has access to your computer and you have an Internet history that you'd rather they not know about, or if you have engaged in any illegal activity over the Internet and you're afraid the law will use that as evidence against you should you ever get accused of such a crime. This is contrary to what many popular Internet advertisements for such software declare with such urgency and extreme exaggeration, such as the popular Internet advertisement shown in Figure 4-3.

Internet Explorer allows you to control how often it compares the information it has already stored with information the web page currently contains. You can instruct Internet Explorer to check for these changes in several ways:

- Every time you visit a web page

- Any time you start Internet Explorer

- Decide automatically when the files need to be updated

- Never check for changes and always load the stored (also referred to as *cached*) files from the temporary Internet files section of your hard disk

You can also instruct Internet Explorer to delete all temporary Internet files and even specify a maximum amount of hard disk space that those files can never exceed.

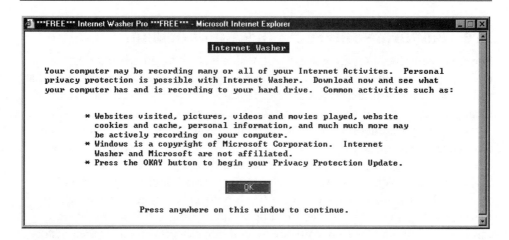

**FIGURE 4-3**    Typical Internet advertisement encouraging needless paranoia

## Taking Control of Your Temporary Internet Files

To optimize your temporary Internet file storage settings, follow these steps:

1. For Windows 98/Me, click **Start**, click **Settings**, and click **Control Panel**. For Windows XP, click **Start** and click **Control Panel**.

2. Double-click the icon labeled **Internet Options**.

3. The General page opens. Click the **Delete Files…** button, which is in the middle of the page, under **Temporary Internet files** (see Figure 4-2).

4. Place a check in the box next to **Delete all offline content** and click **OK**. (This process may take a few minutes, depending on how large your temporary Internet file area is and the speed of your computer.)

5. Click the **Settings** button.

6. In the Settings dialog box, ensure the option **Automatically** is selected and set the maximum amount of disk space to be used to **30**MB. Your screen should now look like Figure 4-4.

7. Click **OK**, and then close the Control Panel.

FIGURE 4-4    Temporary Internet files settings

# Internet Pop-ups

An Internet *pop-up* is typically an advertisement that appears in a new browser window on your screen. It can be quite annoying when these smaller, advertising-based windows cover portions of a legitimate window you are attempting to view.

In many cases, when you attempt to close one or more of these Internet pop-up windows, they can trigger other pop-up windows to appear, causing extreme frustration. This is all thanks to JavaScript, a computer programming language invented to enhance Internet web pages.

> NOTE  *JavaScript code is placed inside a normal web page. When people view that web page, their browser's (Internet Explorer and Netscape are examples of browsers) built-in interpreter reads the JavaScript and runs it. JavaScript can be used for accomplishing many different tasks. One popular way JavaScript is used is to gather information from users in online forms. In this case, JavaScript can help validate entries. For example, a programmer might want to validate a person's age entry falls between 10 and 100.*

Recently, new forms of advertising using a pop-up-like mentality started to surface across the Internet. There are now *pop-unders*, which work like pop-ups, except they hide behind your main window, waiting until you close it to bombard you with their advertisements.

## Popping the Pop-ups!

You can prevent pop-ups and pop-unders from ever opening and, once again, you don't need to spend a penny on ad-blocker software to do it! Since the pop-ups and pop-unders require JavaScript to run, you simply need to turn off JavaScript.

Unfortunately, this results in problems with many web pages that rely on JavaScript. Fortunately, Internet Explorer has a wonderful system of Internet security settings that can allow you to group pages into categories and apply different settings to those categories. We will show you, first, how to disable JavaScript. Then you'll learn how to instruct the computer to allow JavaScript only for web sites that you specify.

### Disabling JavaScript

1. For Windows 98/Me, click **Start**, click **Settings**, and click **Control Panel**. For Windows XP, click **Start** and click **Control Panel**.

2. Double-click the **Internet Options** icon.

3.  Click the tab labeled **Security**.

4.  Ensure **Internet** is selected at the top of window as shown in Figure 4-5, and then click the button labeled **Custom Level…**

5.  Choose every **DISABLE** option in the window that opens as shown in Figure 4-6, and then click **OK** and click **OK** once more. Now you have just disabled every possible means that a web site has to force a pop-up or pop-under advertisement on your PC.

6.  To test this, visit a web site that you know has pop-up advertising. For example, if you take a moment right now to visit www.tripod.com, you'll see no pop-up or pop-under window appears.

Eventually, you will discover that some pages you want to use, such as www.hotmail.com or www.windowsupdate.com, will no longer function properly. If this happens, simply add those web sites to your Trusted Sites list.

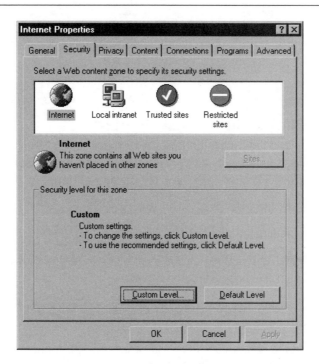

FIGURE 4-5   Internet Security options dialog window

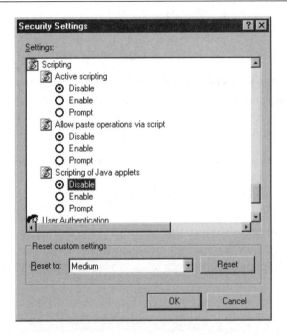

**FIGURE 4-6**   Disable all options in the Security Settings window

## Adding Web Sites to the Trusted Sites List

1. For Windows 98/Me, click **Start**, click **Settings**, and click **Control Panel**. For Windows XP, click **Start** and click **Control Panel**.

2. Double-click the **Internet Options** icon.

3. Click the tab labeled **Security**.

4. Ensure **Trusted Sites** is selected at the top of window, as shown in Figure 4-7, and then click the button labeled **Sites...**

5. *Uncheck* the box that says **Require server verification (https:) for all sites in this zone**, as shown in Figure 4-8.

6. To instruct the computer which web sites are safe, simply enter them in the space provided next to **Add this Web site to the zone:**

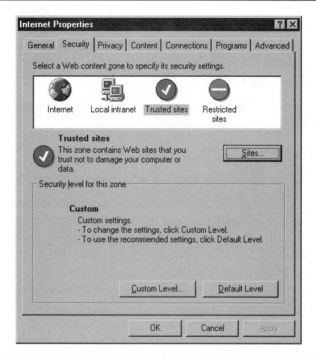

**FIGURE 4-7**    Selecting Trusted Sites in the Internet Security options dialog window

**FIGURE 4-8**    Using the Trusted Sites window to add or remove web sites that you wish to allow JavaScript functionality

**7.** When entering a trusted web site, leave out the information that appears before the first period. For example, if you wanted to add www.hotmail.com to your trusted sites list, simply type hotmail.com in the space provided and click the button labeled **Add**. To add www.windowsupdate.com, you would enter windowsupdate.com and click **Add**.

**8.** If you want to test this, add tripod.com to your trusted sites list and then click **OK**.

**9.** Next, visit www.tripod.com and a pop-up should appear. If so, you've done everything correctly!

Additionally, some sites like www.hotmail.com actually reroute you all over the place in the process of verifying your user name and password. So, to use your Hotmail account, you will also need to add passport.com to your list of trusted sites. To use windowsupdate.com, you will also need to include microsoft.com to your list of Trusted Sites.

This may be a little confusing at first, but it virtually eliminates all pop-up and pop-under advertisements. Occasionally, you will realize that a link is not taking you somewhere or a web site does not load completely or loads with an error message. If this happens, simply add the site to your Trusted Sites list and try accessing it again.

## Removing Web Sites from the Trusted Sites list

To remove any web site that you have entered by mistake or have simply changed your mind about, simply go back to the Security settings as described in Steps 1-5 above. After you have clicked the **Sites...** button, a window will appear with a list of all of your trusted sites. Internet Explorer will automatically put a "*" in front of all of the web site names you have entered, as in **\*.tripod.com**. The asterisk (\*), also referred to as a *wildcard*, tells the computer that any URL ending in hotmail.com will be trusted.

Click once on any site in the list that you no longer wish to trust and then click the **Remove** button. Continue this process, one at a time, for each site you want to remove.

If you added tripod.com to your trusted sites list, as recommended in the previous steps, go ahead and remove it from the Trusted Sites list now. When you are finished, click **OK** and then click **OK** once more. Next, visit www.tripod.com and no pop-up or pop-under windows should appear.

As if pop-up and pop-under appearances weren't frustrating enough, they can also cause a slowdown in your Internet responsiveness. This is because they use the Internet bandwidth you're paying for to download their text, graphics, and even movies onto your computer, all in an effort to advertise their products! Not only that, but very aggressive pop-up and pop-under window attacks can consume all of your available resources, causing your computer to crash, resulting in possible lost productivity, data, and time.

## For Windows XP Users: Getting Rid of Messenger Pop-Ups

Another twist is the Windows Messenger pop-up advertisement, which started to appear in November 2002. This type of pop-up exploits a tool included with Windows XP intended to allow system administrators (computer gurus at work) to easily send messages to users (employees using the work computers) on their network. Windows Messenger pop-up advertisements are easily discernible from other types of pop-ups because they always show **Messenger Service** at the very top of the window, such as in the example shown in Figure 4-9.

If you like to play games on your computer, there is nothing worse than being kicked out of a game and back onto your Windows desktop because of a Windows Messenger alert!

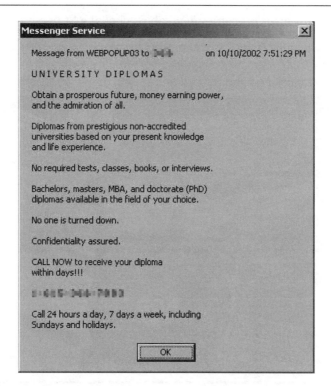

**FIGURE 4-9**    An example of a Windows Messenger pop-up advertisement

So, is there anything you can do? Yes, and like many of the other solutions offered in this book, it won't cost you a cent! There is no need to purchase any software to block Windows Messenger pop-ups. (If you are running Windows 98 or Me, you are not affected by this and can safely skip these steps.)

NOTE    *Many Microsoft products share a common name, such as Windows 2000, Office 2000, and Windows Millennium. Just as Windows Explorer, used for navigating the contents of your disk, shouldn't be confused with Internet Explorer, Windows Messenger shouldn't be confused with MSN Messenger.*

To disable Windows Messenger on a Windows XP computer, follow these steps:

1. Click **Start**, click **Control Panel**, and double-click **Administrative Tools**.

2. Double-click **Services**, as shown in Figure 4-10.

3. Scroll down and double-click **Messenger** (the list should be in alphabetical order), as shown in Figure 4-11.

4. In the Messenger Properties dialog box, click the **Stop** button.

5. Select **Disabled** from the **Startup type** drop-down list, as shown in Figure 4-12.

FIGURE 4-10    Windows XP Administrative Tools window

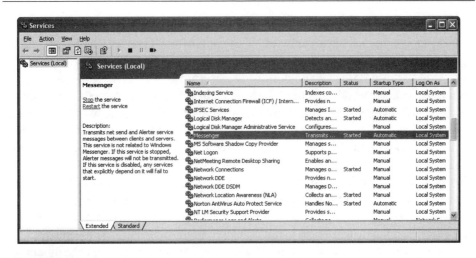

FIGURE 4-11    Windows XP Services window

**6.** Click OK.

You are now blocking Windows Messenger pop-up advertisements forever!

FIGURE 4-12    Windows XP Messenger Properties dialog box

## Summary

In this chapter, you've taken the bytes out of cookies and Java, yet you haven't even had a thing to eat or drink! You've taken control of your Internet experience and put a stop to those intrusive and pesky advertisers. You've learned how to erase your Internet history and even limit the amount of Internet history your computer will store. Ultimately, you've learned you don't need to throw money at a problem in order to solve it; all you really need to know is what keys to press and in what order.

At this point in the book, don't be surprised if you should suddenly feel a strong desire to watch Star Trek, as your understanding of becoming a complete nerd blossoms. Give in to it; resistance is futile. (If you didn't get that last line, you're not a true geek yet, but I guarantee you are closer now than you've ever been!)

I hope you're still hungry, because in the next chapter, we're about to dish out the spam. You're going to learn how to not only prevent unwanted e-mail advertisements, but also how to identify hoax e-mail messages before passing them onto others.

# Chapter 5

## All About Email: Spam and Hoaxes

When the Internet was new, not many people were using it, and many businesses never considered the idea of using the Internet as a means to market their products. But as more and more people got connected to the Internet, businesses began to realize the enormous potential it held as a marketing and selling tool. The trend started with advertising in online forums, then web pages, and eventually led up to pummeling your email inbox with messages about anything anyone could possibly sell.

To make matters worse, some people find it amusing to spread false information in email messages disguised as calls for help, public safety warnings, or easy ways to make money. There are also email chain letters. And, as you've already learned, many virus creators like to use email as a means to transport their viruses from one machine to another.

In this chapter, you'll learn how to spot email hoaxes and not become a victim of someone's practical joke. You'll also learn how to teach your computer to sort your email for you, separating the legitimate email you want to read from the junk email you never asked for.

## Email Hoaxes

Email hoaxes are a modern version of urban legend, or folklore, stories. When I was growing up as a child, we were told to be careful of any apples we received while trick-or-treating during Halloween. Apparently, as the story goes, some people were putting razor blades in apples, making them hazardous to eat. The *New York Times* (10/28/70, page 56) and even the "Dear Abby" column mentioned this potential threat to concerned parents. Years later, researchers Joel Best and Gerald Horiuchi studied national crime data from 1958 to 1985. They did not find a single reported incident of a razor appearing in an apple, or any other fruit or candy for that matter. The children who were harmed by tainted candy, as reported during those years, were harmed by members of their own family.

I mention this story because the Internet has created a new and fast way for the distribution of information. Some of this information is really nothing more than misinformation written by pranksters who get a kick from seeing how gullible people can be. Although hoaxes aren't as directly harmful as viruses or Trojans, they can be time-consuming and costly. Email hoaxes not only consume Internet bandwidth, but they are also responsible for the combined lost productivity of those who take the time to read the message and then perpetuate the hoax by forwarding it to others, who in turn, repeat this cycle.

A very popular Internet email hoax that still circulates encourages people to delete a file called JDBGMGR.EXE from their computers. The email warns that no antivirus software can detect this nasty virus, and you must manually delete this file if it exists on your hard disk. The email is even so kind as to walk you through the necessary steps to locate and remove this file. It encourages you to forward the message to others, so that they can remove this "virus" as well.

The problem is that the file JDBGMGR.EXE is a legitimate Windows file (although one you will probably never miss). For some reason, Microsoft associated a little cartoon bear icon with the file. If you followed the hoax email message instructions (which reference that cute bear icon) and delete this file, it is not necessary to recover it unless you develop Java programs using Microsoft's Visual J++ 1.1.

If you receive this email message, delete it, and do not forward it to others. Although the file mentioned may have the possibility of being infected with a virus, its presence is not an indication of a virus infection.

## How Can I Tell a Hoax from a Legitimate Message?

Hoax email messages generally contain a subject that grabs your attention such as "Free Money" or "IMPORTANT: PLEASE READ!!!" or "Virus Alert." Within the message is usually a threat of some sort of repercussion if you do not take appropriate action. It may say files are going to be deleted, you will lose money, or you will have bad luck. Some even go so far as to mention a reward of cash or a cute animation on your screen as payment for your participation.

Finally, the hoax will contain a request. There can be any number of possible requests, but the one that gives it away as a hoax is the insistence that you pass the message along, or *forward*, it to others. A perfect example of this is shown in Figure 5-1. Certainly, someone could send you a legitimate message asking you to forward it to others, but most of time, these requests are just perpetuating hoaxes.

In general, a hoax tends to leave out specific information, and that's what makes it effective. If you say the world may end sometime soon, you're more likely to be believed than if you state the world will end at midnight, January 1, 2004.

Some people think it's better to be safe than sorry (as implied in the message shown in Figure 5-1) and use that justification to forward a hoax email message to others. Using that same logic, would you yell "FIRE!" in a crowded theater, simply because you felt a little warm?

If you aren't sure if a message is a hoax, there are web sites you can check that are dedicated to eradicating such hoaxes and increasing public awareness:

■   http://hoaxbusters.ciac.org

- http://www.nonprofit.net/hoax

- http://www.truthorfiction.com

- http://www.vmyths.com

- http://www.symantec.com/avcenter/hoax.html

- http://www.stiller.com/hoaxa.htm

- http://snopes.com

- http://www.urbanlegends.com

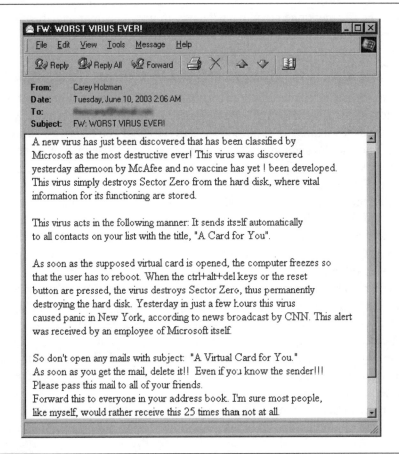

**FIGURE 5-1**    An example of a common email hoax message

These are just some of the hundreds of web sites dedicated to dispelling email hoaxes. Use any of these web sites to help determine if an email message you received is a hoax before irresponsibly passing it along to others.

## What Else Should I Know About Email Hoaxes?

In general, you should know that there is no such thing as an email-tracking program and no company will pay you for forwarding messages. No virus can cause hardware damage. Although viruses can potentially cause the loss or corruption of data on your computer, they can never cause any permanent hardware failure. No animations will appear on your screen, and you will never receive anything in return for forwarding an email. Since there is no way for an outside source to track your email, no one can know that you sent it except for the people who received it from you.

Be aware that there is no bill in Congress to place a tax on email, there was never a Neiman-Marcus cookie recipe, and there have never been tainted needles found on gas station pumps or in children's play areas. There is no virus you need to manually delete from your computer because antivirus software cannot detect it (as long as you keep your antivirus software up to date!).

Hotmail, Yahoo, ICQ, and other services will never demand that you send messages to verify that your account is active. Simply logging on to those services allows them to determine whether or not your account is active. Credit card companies will *never* ask you for *any* personal information via email. Microsoft will *never* send you an email with an attachment. If you receive an email from Microsoft that supposedly contains an update or screensaver, delete it immediately.

Finally, there is no poison perfume, your email address is NOT expiring, nor is there such a thing as a virus-infected message with the subject "WTC Survivor."

# Spam

*Spam* is geek terminology for unsolicited junk email and messages. Spam is fast becoming a huge problem. It's starting to cost corporations millions of dollars each year to filter out spam, and handling spam has required companies to increase their server storage space and Internet bandwidth for all the extra traffic it generates.

## Why Do I Receive So Many Spam Messages?

Once you give out your email address to a company, it may be sold to other companies. Those other companies quite often sell your email address to other companies, and

## Why Is It Called Spam?

Spam is actually a canned meat product made by Hormel, which is widely available in the United States and other countries (see www.spam.com for details).

The term *spam* originated from an old British comedy troupe called Monty Python. (Generally speaking, computer nerds love Monty Python.) One of their more famous sketches included a husband and wife who visit a restaurant in which everything on the menu contains Spam as an ingredient. As the waitress is explaining all the Spam-enhanced meals to the husband and wife, a group of men dressed as Vikings start singing about Spam. The wife says she doesn't like Spam, and she attempts to ask the waitress if the restaurant has anything available that does not contain Spam. Unfortunately, the Vikings start singing louder and louder, drowning out everyone around them with their loud voices. (This may not sound funny to you unless you understand British humor.)

The first encounters of spam messages were in online discussion forums, known as *newsgroups*. As large amounts of unwanted advertisements (in many cases, the same advertisements repeated over and over) interrupted the normal flow of conversation, it made further discussion difficult or even impossible. Many people who were affected by this remembered the Monty Python skit about Spam, where the characters sing Spam so often and so loudly that other people in the restaurant cannot carry on a conversation. Thus, everyone started referring to these junk messages as "spam."

Initially, some people wanted to give junk email an official name, such as UCE (unsolicited commercial email) or UBE (unsolicited bulk email). But the term *spam* stuck, perhaps because it's easier to remember or because so many computer nerds are fans of Monty Python and understood the reference. I doubt that the Hormel folks are happy with the term, but there's not much they can do about it.

so on into infinity. The following are some of the most common ways people unwittingly offer their email addresses to companies:

- Filling out online registration forms
- Entering contests
- Engaging in online discussion groups
- Filling out online surveys
- Choosing a common name for your email address

■ If you belong to America Online (AOL), having a member profile and/or participating in chat rooms

Also, some companies use a method called a *dictionary attack*. They compile many common names to form a list, or *dictionary of names*, and then mix names from this list with a list of arbitrary *domain names* in the reasonable expectation that some of the resulting combinations will be valid.

> **NOTE** *To put it simply, a domain name is the information that follows the @ symbol in any email address. Examples of domain names are aol.com and hotmail.com.*

## Is There Anything I Can Do About Spam?

Once you start receiving spam, it is practically impossible to put a stop to it without changing your email address. Some Internet service providers (ISPs) have started to *filter* spam messages before they reach you; however, automating a process to decipher an unwanted advertisement from a wanted advertisement is practically impossible. Some advertising messages are legitimate, and you may have even requested that they be sent to you. For example, you may ask a retailer to send you an email concerning any upcoming specials or sales. Your ISP cannot determine if the message sent had your prior approval. As a result, many spam messages are not intercepted by your ISP.

> **NOTE** *The process of automating the detection and removal of spam from legitimate email is referred to as filtering.*

Some spam messages offer you the option to be taken off of their email list. In most cases, when you respond to these messages, your request doesn't go through, because the address they are directing you to is fake. Other times, when your request does go through, they use it as verification that you received their email advertisement. Now they know you are receiving and reading their messages, which makes your email address even more valuable to them (as well as to other companies that they may sell it to). Only if the email comes from a large, reputable company or if you previously requested to be sent email advertisements should you ever request to be removed from a mailing list.

You can enable filtering for all of your email by setting rules and restrictions in your email software. With the filters configured to your preferences, your email software can automatically decide which email messages you want to receive and which messages you want to ignore. This process varies depending on the software you use to check your email. Here, I'll explain how to filter email messages with some of the most popular software: AOL, Microsoft Outlook, Microsoft Outlook Express, NetZero, Hotmail, and Yahoo.

## Enabling Filters Using AOL 8.0 Plus

AOL has a feature called Mail Controls. You can use this feature to filter email, as follows:

1. Access the Mail Controls by logging in to AOL with your master screen name (the first screen name you created when you joined AOL, if you have more than one) and go to your email inbox in AOL.

2. Click **Mail Options** (located at the top of the screen) and select **Block Unwanted Mail**.

3. You will see that AOL offers three options: Allow all email to be delivered to this Screen Name, Block all email from being delivered to this Screen Name, and Customize Mail Controls for this Screen Name. Select **Customize** and click **Next.**

4. In the screen that appears, shown in Figure 5-2, you can choose to block email from entire Internet domain names or specify individual email addresses. You can also choose to block email containing files or pictures. If you constantly receive pornographic advertisements, choosing to block pictures will prevent those images from being displayed. Blocking files prevents the possibility of having your computer infected by a virus. However, enabling this option means legitimate files and pictures will be inaccessible to you. Once you have finished making your selections, click **Summary,** and then click **Save**.

For additional information, click the **Mail Controls Help** button at the top of the Mail Controls screen. You can also call AOL technical support to get answers to any questions you may have concerning this feature.

NOTE    *AOL is a proprietary system. There is no alternative method to check your email other than using the software provided by AOL or by visiting www.aol.com. As of the writing of this book, it is not, and has never been, possible to configure any dedicated email program (such as Microsoft Outlook Express or Microsoft Outlook) to work with AOL.*

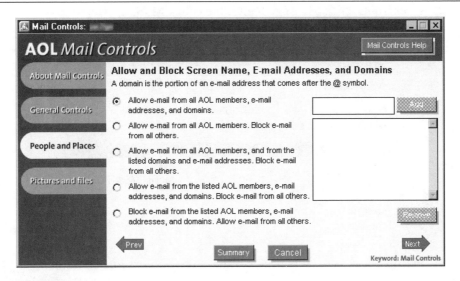

**FIGURE 5-2**   Using AOL 8.0 Plus Mail Controls to filter email

## Enabling Filters Using Microsoft Outlook or Outlook Express

Microsoft likes to refer to its mail filters as *rules*. You can configure the email rules in a number of different ways.

Microsoft Outlook is a feature-rich version of Outlook Express that is included with Microsoft Office. Microsoft Outlook Express is included free with all versions of Windows. Both products can sort or filter your email based on the sender, the subject, a specific word anywhere in the message, or numerous other possibilities.

Since all Windows users have Outlook Express and because Outlook operates in a very similar fashion, the following example uses Outlook Express.

If you want to send all email messages that contain the word Viagra in the subject of the message to the Deleted Items folder, follow these easy steps:

1. Open Outlook Express.

2. Click **Tools**, click **Message Rules**, then click **Mail**.

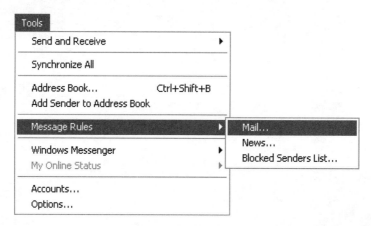

3. Place a check in the box next to **Where the Subject line contains specific words**.

4. Place a check in the box next to **Move it to the specified folder**.

5. In the rule description, you will see underlined words. Clicking on these words allows you to enter the specific information about this new rule. As shown in Figure 5-3, click once on **contains specific words**. In the dialog box that opens, type in **Viagra** and click the **Add** button, as shown in Figure 5-4. You can continue to add other words at this time if you choose. At this point, you are telling Outlook Express to apply this rule to any message that contains any one of the words you enter if found in the subject of the message. When you are finished, click **OK**.

6. Next, click on **specified** and click the + symbol next to Folders to display all of your Outlook Express email folders. Select the Deleted Items folder and click **OK** (see Figure 5-5).

7. Finally, the last step is to give the rule a name. We'll call this one **Delete Unwanted Mail**. Just type that in, or any other name that you wish, and then click **OK**.

The window that appears will show you all of your rules, and by selecting any rule, the description window will show underlined words that will allow you to add or remove or modify the rules settings at any point in the future. Click **OK** to complete this task.

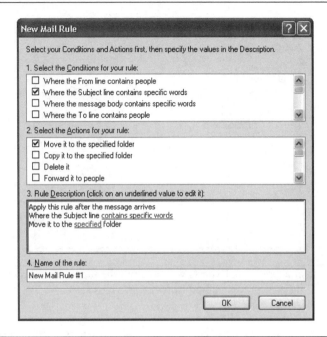

Finding the mail rules in Outlook Express version 6

From now on, as new mail arrives, the filter will check the subject of all incoming email and send any messages containing the word Viagra immediately to your Deleted Items folder.

Enter words you want Outlook Express to watch for.

**FIGURE 5-5**   Instruct Outlook Express where to put the messages that contain any one of the words you entered from the previous step.

This process won't solve your spam problems entirely, however. That's because many spammers will misspell words on purpose. For the same reason, it's probably a waste of your time to create a filter to automatically send unwanted email messages from specific senders to the Deleted Items folder because most spammers never use the same "from" address more than once.

You may have noticed that the option to Delete Item was available in the rules options. Selecting that box accomplishes the same goal; however, I chose to walk you through this process in a manner that will make you familiar with how the rules work. You can create new folders and call them anything you wish and send specific messages from specific people or groups of people into those specific folders, effectively allowing Outlook or Outlook Express to sort your email for you automatically and not just spam.

For a more detailed tutorial on using the filter options in Outlook Express, start Outlook Express and press the F1 key on your keyboard. Type in the word **rules**. Click any of the related topics to learn how to configure email rules.

There is a free utility that integrates with the rules settings of Outlook and Outlook Express and automates the spam removal process. This software is called POPFile and was created by John Graham-Cumming. (John is a programmer who has the desire to help others and finances his work through donations.) You can download this software, as well as find detailed instructions on how to install and configure it, at http://popfile.sourceforge.net.

In simple terms, the POPFile software maintains a memory of words commonly found in classes (known as "buckets") you have set up (one bucket might be called SPAM while another might be called REGULAR) and judges incoming email messages based on the probabilities of that email containing specific words belonging to each class. It then marks the email as a member of whichever class comes out with the highest probability and associates it with the appropriate bucket.

A great web site that further explains the setup and use of POPFile (should you require more assistance) can be found at http://www.tames.net/security/popfile.htm.

### Enabling Filters Using NetZero

The free version of NetZero does not have any email filter options. However, you can configure Microsoft Outlook Express or Microsoft Outlook to check your NetZero email. Then you can use the filtering techniques described in the previous section for Microsoft Outlook or Microsoft Outlook Express.

To learn how to configure Microsoft Outlook or Outlook Express to check your NetZero email, visit www.netzero.net/support/email/email-setup.html.

### Enabling Filters Using Hotmail

To enable filters using Hotmail, after you've signed in to Hotmail, click **Options** at the top of the screen. Under the heading **Mail Handling**, there are several self-explanatory options for controlling how your email is handled.

Alternatively, you can configure Hotmail to work with Microsoft Outlook Express and use the filter options available in Outlook Express.

Because Hotmail does not use something called a *POP3 server,* the free POPFile software, which automates the spam-removal process for Outlook and Outlook Express, will not work with Hotmail.

NOTE *POP is short for Post Office Protocol and is the standard method most Internet Service Providers (ISPs) use to allow you to retrieve your email from their servers. Services such as AOL are considered "closed systems" because you must use their proprietary software to read your email. POP3 allows you to download your mail on to your computer using a program that supports POP3, such as Outlook or Outlook Express. If you open Internet Explorer to read your email, this is referred to as web-based email. Most free email services such as Yahoo require that you use Internet Explorer to check your email. There are pros and cons to each of these methods; however, the only method that allows you to save your email on your computer automatically is POP3.*

### Enabling Filters Using Yahoo

If you use Yahoo to check your email, you can filter email by following these steps:

1.  Sign in to your Yahoo email account and click **Mail Options**. This appears in two places on your screen: on the upper-right side and also on the lower-right side. Clicking either one will work equally well.

2.  In the center of the screen, under the heading **Management**, click the **Filters** link. Here, you can customize how you would like Yahoo to handle and direct your email.

I recommend reading the section titled **Avoiding Spam,** located under the **Help** link in the upper-right corner of the screen.

# Summary

In this chapter, you've learned how to tell an email hoax from a legitimate message. You've also learned why spam is so prevalent on the Internet, why it's called spam, and how to prevent most of it from appearing in your email inbox. You're doing great!

In the next chapter, you'll learn what a firewall is and why you'll probably want one (if you're not using one already).

# Chapter 6

## Firewalls

An unprotected computer with a high-speed Internet connection is not only irresponsible and inconsiderate to other Internet users, but it can also be the cause of frustration to the owner of the infected computer because of its reduced performance and reliability. In this chapter, you'll learn all about firewalls and how you can ensure that your computer is not being controlled by outside forces to do bad things to other people's computers on the Internet without your knowledge or consent.

When you're on the Internet, it's possible for people to "break in" to your computer and view, alter, steal, or even delete files from your computer without your knowledge. In fact, many people who have unprotected high-speed Internet connections are unknowingly responsible for the spread of viruses, distributed denial of service (DDoS) attacks and even sending out spam. Having your computer on a high-speed Internet connection without proper protection is no different than voluntarily handing your computer over to a stranger.

## What Is a DDoS Attack?

A distributed denial of service (DDoS) attack occurs when someone commandeers several hundred, or even thousand, computers and instructs them to access a particular web site at the same time. This typically happens with PCs that are infected with a kind of virus that opens a *backdoor* to your computer. A backdoor is computer language for a secret entrance. Any computer can have a virus or Trojan that installs this backdoor, giving full access to anyone who knows how to look for it. The web site cannot respond to all of the simultaneous requests and, as a result, a "page not found" error will occur. When this is done for hours or days at a time, it can prevent legitimate visitors from accessing that web page.

What if I could remotely control the telephones of a hundred people, and I instructed those telephones to dial your telephone number over and over for hours on end? When your telephone rings, how do you determine if there is a legitimate caller on the other end of the line without answering it? In the meantime, everyone else that is trying to call you during this time, legitimate or not, will get a busy signal. The best you can do is answer the phone as quickly and as often as you can, and hope the people who call and get a busy signal will try again. Now, imagine this happening to a business telephone number for an incoming sales line. Then you can begin to understand the serious implications a DDoS attack can have on a web site.

# What Is a Firewall?

Think of a firewall as you would an alarm for your house. Think of antivirus software as you would pesticide for your home. Now, the alarm system won't keep out the bugs, and the pesticide won't keep out the burglars. That is why it's important that your computer has both a firewall and antivirus software running at all times!

> **NOTE**  *The dictionary defines a firewall as a barrier to prevent the spread of fire. In computer terms, a firewall can be any of a number of security schemes that prevent unauthorized users from gaining access to a computer network. A firewall is also commonly used to monitor the transfer of data in and out of a network.*

## Aren't Firewalls Complicated and Expensive?

Most firewalls designed for home users are incredibly easy to use. A firewall can be hardware or software. Some firewall software may contain numerous other features as well. For example, Symantec's Norton Internet Security (www.symantec.com) has the following key features:

- **Parental Control**   Used to block unsuitable web sites so that you can rest easy when your children are surfing the Internet.

- **AntiVirus**   Yes, firewall and antivirus in the same software package! What a concept!

- **Spam Alert**   Used to block unwanted email messages from reaching your inbox.

- **Ad Blocking**   Used to help put a stop to banner ads, pop-ups, and pop-under advertising windows.

- **Privacy Control**   Used to prevent information being sent from your computer without your permission.

- **Connection Keep Alive**   Used to help prevent dial-up Internet sessions from being disconnected due to periods of inactivity.

- **Web Cleanup**   Used to delete unneeded files left over from Internet sessions.

- **Cookie Control**   Used to accept or reject a cookie any time a web site attempts to create one to your computer.

Other firewall software packages, like Zone Labs Zone Alarm (www.zonelabs .com) or Tiny Software's Tiny Personal Firewall (www.tinysoftware.com), offer fantastic firewall protection. These vendors offer their basic, sometimes called *personal*, firewall product to home users for free.

## What About Hardware Firewalls?

An example of the most common type of a consumer-based hardware firewall is included with the purchase of a consumer *router*. A consumer-based router usually does the job of two, three, and sometimes even four devices. A consumer-based router allows you to share most high-speed Internet connections among as many as 253 computers (assuming you have that many ports available). For as little as $50, a basic consumer router will have four ports (think of a *port* as a socket that you can plug your computer into) that will allow up to four computers to simultaneously and independently share your high-speed Internet connection without needing to pay your ISP any additional fees, ever.

NOTE   *A distinction is made between a router intended for consumers and one intended for businesses. The explanations offered here are for consumer-based routers only. These routers are designed with numerous, easy-to-use features intended for the home and small office user. Large corporations have different requirements than consumers. The routers they use serve a different purpose than what is explained here, cost a lot more money, and require much more technical knowledge to configure.*

A router is always connected to at least two networks, typically a local area network (LAN) and a wide area network (WAN), with your home being the LAN and the Internet being the WAN. The router intelligently decides how to direct data from one computer to another based on its current understanding of the state of the networks to which it's connected. The router's job is to recognize and differentiate all of the computers on your network from other computers not on your network.

We refer to computers located in the same building as being a local area network or LAN. When we need to go miles (whether it's one or 20,000 miles) between two or more computers that are communicating with each other, we call that a wide area network or WAN.

In addition, a consumer router acts as a *switch*. A switch is a device that controls and directs communication between two or more computers. Think of a switch as a traffic cop. This is useful because it can allow the sharing of files and printers between the computers if the user chooses to share those things. That means that any computer can have access to any files and print to any printer attached to any other computer on the network. (Any computers plugged into a switch would be considered a network, or more specifically, a LAN.)

> **NOTE** *Generally speaking, you cannot share programs over a LAN or WAN, only the data. For example, if you have a Microsoft Word document on one PC, you can access it from another PC if those PCs are networked together and each has its own copy of Microsoft Word.*

A consumer-based router usually includes a firewall as well, to ensure that no one on the Internet can access your files or print to your printers.

Some routers even come with a built-in *print server*. A print server is nothing more than a standard printer socket (the same as the one on the back of your PC) located on the router, designed for plugging in your printer. Then, any computer that is connected to the router can print to that printer. You can always share a printer on a network, but in order for others to be able to print to it, the computer that the printer is physically attached to must be powered on. By plugging the printer directly into the router, you make the printer available at all times to anyone on the LAN.

## Wireless Routers

Routers are now available in wireless versions, such as the one shown in Figure 6-1. Just like a cordless phone, this enables you to share your Internet connection, files, and printers with other computers in your house (maybe even your neighbor's house, if you so choose) without needing to run or install any wires.

A wireless router will also act as a regular, wired router. If a wireless router is available for a few dollars more, I would recommend purchasing it, even if you have no immediate need for the wireless portion. This gives you more flexibility in the future, in case your computing needs change. Just because you have a router that has wireless capabilities doesn't mean you need to use the wireless aspect of the router. It will function exactly the same as a wired router, if that's how you choose to use it.

There are several different standards for wireless routers to communicate with wireless network cards. The current standards are 802.11b, 802.11a, and 802.11g. The letters represent the frequency and bandwidth the router communicates with. The 802.11b standard is the slowest, and it is also the cheapest. Even the slowest wireless connection will usually be ten times faster than the average high-speed Internet connection. Whichever wireless standard you choose, it's recommended that you purchase all your wireless products from the same company to make installation and configuration as simple, reliable, and straightforward as possible.

FIGURE 6-1    The front and back of a wireless SMC router, model 7004AWBR
(picture courtesy of SMC)

### How Difficult Is a Hardware Router to Set Up?

Most routers available today are Plug and Play. In much the same way that a
telephone answering machine is wired between your telephone and a wall socket,
a router is simply wired between your computer(s) and your cable/DSL/satellite
modem, as illustrated in Figure 6-2.

In most cases, the router will automatically configure itself once it is turned on.
This varies based on the router you purchase and your high-speed ISP's requirements.
Most routers come with a quick-installation guide, separate from the detailed and
lengthy documentation, to get you up and running as quickly and painlessly as
possible. I recommend SMC, D-Link, Netgear, and Hawking networking products
(in that order). They are inexpensive, widely available, easy to install, and very
reliable.

## I Was Told Windows XP Includes a Firewall!

Windows XP does, in fact, come with a firewall. However, it's a very basic and
rigid firewall, with few options to configure it. It's certainly better than nothing,
unless you have a home network. That is because enabling Windows XP's firewall
may prevent other computers on your network from being able to communicate
with it or each other. However, if you have just one PC, and it has Windows XP,
I recommend enabling the built-in firewall.

To enable the Windows XP firewall, follow these steps:

1. Click **Start**, and then click **Control Panel**.

2. Double-click the **Network Connections** icon.

3. Right-click an icon and select **Properties**.

4. Click the **Advanced** tab.

5. Place a check in the box next to **Protect my computer and network by limiting or preventing access to this computer from the Internet**, as shown in Figure 6-3.

6. Click **OK**.

7. Repeat steps 3 through 6 for any other icons in the Network Connections window.

8. Close any remaining open windows.

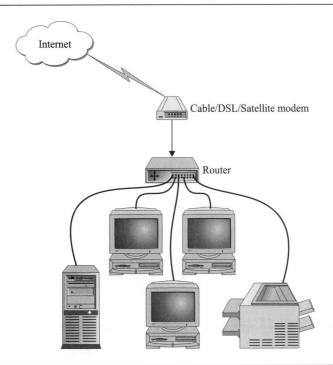

**FIGURE 6-2**   Typical installation of a router

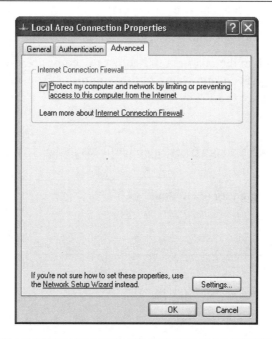

**FIGURE 6-3** Enabling the Windows XP built-in firewall

Once you have completed this process with all the icons listed in the Network Connections window, all of the icons should have a small lock that appears in their upper-right corner, as shown in Figure 6-4.

*Never run two different firewall (or antivirus) programs at the same time. If you decide to use an alternate firewall, be sure to disable the Windows XP built-in firewall and uninstall any previously installed firewall software before installing the replacement. It is okay, however, to have a single hardware and a single software firewall working together.*

## How Can I Tell If My Computer Is Vulnerable?

If you don't think you need a firewall, you're not sure if you have one, or you have installed a firewall and want to see if it is working correctly, there is help available. A gentleman by the name of Steve Gibson has a web site representing his company, Gibson Research Corporation. In it, he offers plenty of computer

**FIGURE 6-4** Local Area Connection icon with the Windows XP firewall enabled

security information and several free utilities. One of these utilities is called ShieldsUP!, which is specifically designed to check for Internet-based vulnerabilities in your computer.

To test your computer with ShieldsUP!, visit www.grc.com and click the **ShieldsUP!** link. Under the section titled "Hot Spots," click the link for ShieldsUP! Follow the onscreen instructions, and be sure to run the Test My Shields! and Probe My Ports! tests.

For more firewall information and reviews of numerous software firewall solutions, visit www.firewallguide.com.

# Universal Plug and Play

Now that you know about Internet risks and why you need a firewall, you may be wondering if there is anything else you should know. Yes, there is. Both Windows Me and Windows XP include a "feature" called Universal Plug and Play (UPnP). This feature was designed to allow electronic devices to communicate with one another, without requiring a technician to configure everything. These items would include your home stereo, refrigerator, washing machine, and any other device using UPnP technology. Unfortunately, the only devices that currently support UPnP are routers. Since most routers don't need to be configured anyway, UPnP is not particularly useful.

Many people confuse UPnP with regular Plug and Play (PnP). They are two entirely different things. You can read more about UPnP at www.upnp.org.

In December 2001, the FBI's National Infrastructure Protection Center (NIPC) issued a public warning about the vulnerabilities that exist in the UPnP feature included with Windows Me and Windows XP (to read this official government warning, visit www.nipc.gov/warnings/advisories/2001/01-030-2.htm). Therefore, you might want to disable UPnP on your computer.

One option is to use a free utility called UnPlug 'n Pray, available at www.grc.com, that will disable the UPnP service with the click of one button. Alternatively, you can disable this service through the Windows Add/Remove Programs utility.

## Disabling UPnP in Windows Me

To disable UPnP in Windows Me, follow these steps:

1. Click **Start**, click **Settings**, and then click **Control Panel**.

2. Double-click **Add/Remove Programs**.

3. Click the **Windows Setup** tab.

4. Double-click **Communications**, as shown in Figure 6-5.

5. Uncheck **Universal Plug and Play**, as shown in Figure 6-6.

6. Click **OK**.

FIGURE 6-5   Selecting the Communications option in the Windows Setup tab in Windows Me

Universal Plug and Play —

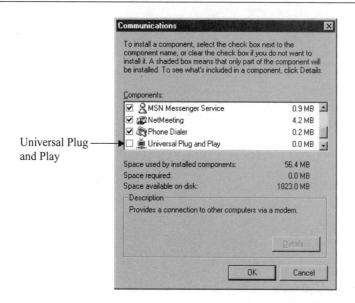

FIGURE 6-6   Disabling Universal Plug and Play in Windows Me

## Disabling UPnP in Windows XP

To disable UPnP in Windows XP, follow these steps:

1. Click **Start**, and then click **Control Panel**.

2. Double-click **Add/Remove Programs**.

3. In the Add or Remove Programs window, shown in Figure 6-7, click the **Add/Remove Windows Components** option on the left side of the window.

4. In the Windows Components window, scroll down to locate **Networking Services**, as shown in Figure 6-8. Then click that item.

5. Click the **Details** button.

6. Locate and uncheck **Universal Plug and Play**, as shown in Figure 6-9.

7. Click **OK**, and then close any remaining windows.

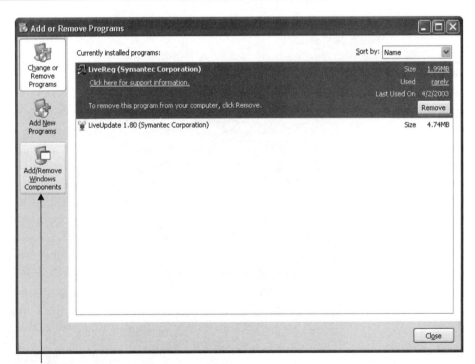

Add/Remove Windows Components button

**FIGURE 6-7**    Choosing the Add/Remove Windows Components option in Windows XP

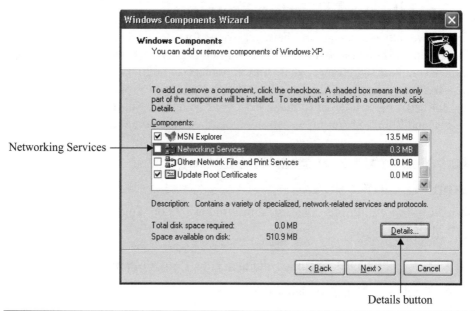

Networking Services —

Details button

**FIGURE 6-8**    Selecting Networking Services in Windows XP

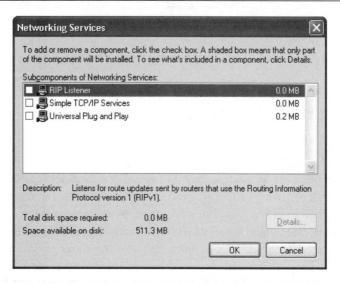

**FIGURE 6-9**    Disabling Universal Plug and Play in Windows XP

# More on File and Printer Sharing

If you have only one computer, there is no need for you to have File and Printer Sharing enabled on your computer. This service is only necessary if you have two or more computers and want to share files or printers (or both) between them. Having this service installed not only consumes needless resources, but it offers another way for bad guys to attempt to break in to your computer. So, if you don't need to use File and Printer Sharing, you can safely remove this service from your computer.

## Removing File and Printer Sharing from Windows 98/Me

To remove File and Printer Sharing from Windows 98 or Windows Me, follow these steps:

1. Click **Start**, click **Settings**, and then click **Control Panel**.

2. Double-click the icon labeled **Network**.

3. Look for **File and printer sharing for Microsoft Networks** at the bottom of the list that appears. If this item is listed, click it, as shown in Figure 6-10. Then click the **Remove** button and click **OK**. (If it isn't listed, just click **Cancel** and close any remaining windows.)

4. If you located and removed the service, you will be asked to restart your computer for the changes to take effect. Click **Yes**.

You have now secured your computer even further from the badness that exists on the Internet.

## Removing Unnecessary Basic Services from Windows XP

Along with File and Printer Sharing, Windows XP has another service that you're even less likely to need as a home user: QoS Packet Scheduler (QoS is short for Quality of Service). This is a tool from Microsoft that enables companies to limit the amount of bandwidth any individual on a network can consume at any given time. Without it, one person using the Internet heavily could slow down everyone else who is sharing the Internet. It's similar to how the water pressure goes down in your home when two or more people crank up the water faucet at the same time (or flush the toilet when you're in the shower). For this service to work, a QoS server must be installed and configured. Since you're a home user, you will not

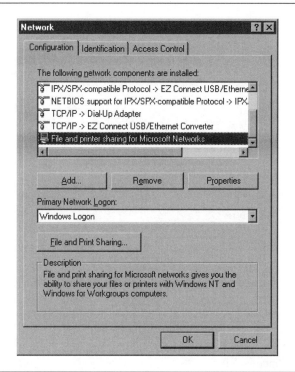

FIGURE 6-10    Removing File and Printer Sharing from Windows 98/Me

have a QoS server, so you do not need this service running and consuming precious resources.

To remove these services from Windows XP, use the following steps:

1. Click **Start**, and then click **Control Panel**.

2. Double-click the icon labeled **Network Connections**.

3. Right-click an icon that appears and select **Properties**.

4. If **File and Printer Sharing for Microsoft Networks** appears in the list, click to select it, as shown in Figure 6-11. Then click the **Uninstall** button. When you're asked if you're sure, click **Yes**.

5. If you see **QoS Packet Scheduler** in the list (as in Figure 6-11), click it, and then click the **Uninstall** button. When you're asked if you're sure, click **Yes**.

6. Click the **Close** button.

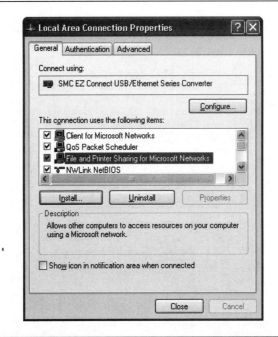

**FIGURE 6-11**    Removing File and Printer Sharing and QoS Packet Scheduler from Windows XP

**7.** Repeat steps 3 through 6 for any other icons in the Network Connections window.

**8.** Close any remaining windows.

That's all there is to it. You have now increased your computer's security and reduced the number of tasks your computer needs to juggle.

# Summary

In this chapter, you've learned how to lock down your computer and make it more secure, so that you're not as vulnerable to Internet bad guys. You've learned why having a firewall is so important and how to check to make sure you're protected any time you're curious. See how easy this is? I knew you could do it!

In the next chapter, you'll learn how to ensure your Windows operating system is configured to run at peak performance. You might be surprised to find how much power your computer has, once you give it permission and instruct it to use all the resources and features that are available.

# Chapter 7

# Basic Windows Performance Tips

There are hidden settings within Windows that tell it how to interact with your particular hardware. These settings, when adjusted properly, can boost your system's performance quite noticeably. Although some of these tweaks may have only a marginal effect, together they can have quite an impact on the speed and reliability with which your computer operates.

Settings you can easily control within Windows can have an adverse effect on how good or bad your operating system runs. In this chapter, you're going to learn about DMA mode, Active Desktop, visual animations, fonts, and swap files. These Windows features can help or hinder you and in these next few pages, you'll learn how to properly configure them.

# DMA Mode

During a typical installation of Windows 98/Me (and sometimes Windows XP), one of its operating system settings is not enabled by default for reliability reasons. Unless your computer was built before 1995, there is no reason that this setting should remain disabled. The setting I am referring to here is called direct memory access (DMA) mode. This setting can have a great impact on your computer performance because it relates to reading and writing data to and from your hard disk.

Rather than enabling DMA mode, the Windows installation program may place your hard disk and/or CD drive(s) in a basic mode called programmed input/output (PIO). A typical computer requires 40 percent of the central processing unit (CPU) to transfer data to a hard disk or CD drive in PIO mode, yet requires only 25 percent of the CPU in DMA mode on the same hardware. Simply by changing this setting, you can reduce the amount of work your computer must do by 15 percent!

DMA mode is sometimes referred to as *bus mastering*, which just means that the disk controller has permission to talk directly to the computer's memory without first going through the CPU. This takes quite a load off of the CPU, which results in better system performance. The terms *direct memory access*, or *DMA*, and *bus mastering* mean the same thing.

You will need to adjust this setting individually for each device you have in your computer. You probably have at least one hard disk and one CD drive. Not all CD drives are compatible with DMA mode, however; most CD-R and CD-RW drives (the drives used to create CDs, sometimes also referred to as *CD burners*) not only support DMA, but will work better, faster, and more reliably with DMA enabled. Enabling DMA mode for your CD drive is the only way to find out if it helps or hinders you.

All of the devices (there won't be more than four on typical home-based PCs) should be compatible with DMA mode. If any one device does not work properly after DMA mode is enabled, you simply need to disable DMA mode for that one device only. Leave DMA mode enabled on the rest of the devices.

NOTE    *If you have any negative effects after restarting your computer once you've enabled DMA mode, you can start the computer in Safe Mode and follow these same steps to disable DMA mode. Activating Safe Mode is explained in detail in Chapter 12.*

## Enabling DMA Mode in Windows 98/Me

To enable DMA mode for your hard disk in Windows 98/Me, follow these steps:

1. Click **Start**, click **Settings**, and then click **Control Panel.**

2. Double-click the **System** icon.

3. Click the tab labeled **Device Manager**.

4. Ensure that the **View devices by type** option at the top of the dialog box is selected, as shown in Figure 7-1.

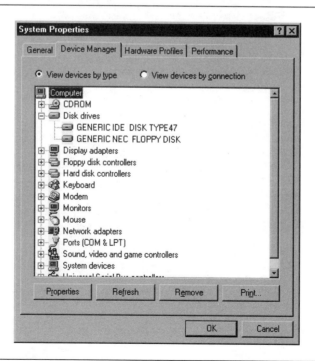

FIGURE 7-1    Device Manager in Windows Me

5. Click the + symbol next to **Disk drives**.

6. Double-click **GENERIC IDE DISK TYPE47** (see Figure 7-1). If more than one hard disk drive is listed, select the first one and complete these steps. Then repeat these steps for the second one.

7. Click the **Settings** tab.

8. If there is not already a check in the box next to **DMA**, as shown in Figure 7-2, click to place one there. If there is already a check in the box next to **DMA**, select **Cancel** and bypass the rest of these steps.

9. After you place a check next to DMA, you will see a warning message similar to the one shown in Figure 7-3 for Windows Me or Figure 7-4 for Windows 98. Because Windows does not know if your hardware supports DMA mode, it automatically assumes it doesn't. Most computers built since 1995 do support DMA mode. Click **OK** to close the dialog box.

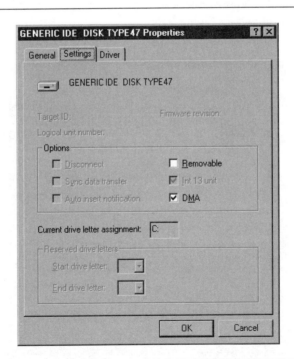

**FIGURE 7-2**   Checking the DMA setting in Windows Me

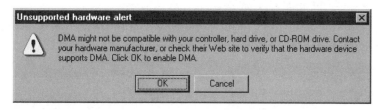

FIGURE 7-3    Windows Me warning about DMA mode support

**10.** Click the **OK** button.

**11.** In Windows Me systems, click the **Close** button.

**12.** You will see a message informing you that you must restart your computer for the change to take effect and asking if you want to restart Windows now. Click **Yes**.

To enable DMA mode for your CD-ROM drive in Windows 98/Me, you follow essentially the same procedure, but choose that drive in Device Manager, as follows:

**1.** Click **Start**, click **Settings**, and then click **Control Panel**.

**2.** Double-click the **System** icon.

**3.** Click the tab labeled **Device Manager**.

**4.** Ensure **View devices by type** is selected (see Figure 7-1).

**5.** Click the + symbol next to **CDROM**.

**6.** Double-click any items that appear. If more than one item is listed, select the first one and complete these steps. Then repeat these steps for the second item.

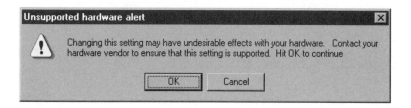

FIGURE 7-4    Windows 98 warning about DMA mode support

7. Click the **Settings** tab.

8. If there is not already a check in the box next to **DMA**, place one there. If there is already a check in the box next to **DMA**, select **Cancel** and bypass the rest of these steps.

9. At the warning message that appears, click **OK**.

10. Click the **OK** button.

11. In Windows Me systems, click the **Close** button.

12. When you see the message about restarting (or shutting down) your computer for the change to take effect, click **Yes**.

## Enabling DMA Mode in Windows XP

*Turned on by default* To enable DMA mode in Windows XP, follow these steps:

1. Click **Start**, and then click **Control Panel**.

2. Double-click the **System** icon.

3. Click the **Hardware** tab.

4. Click the button labeled **Device Manager**.

5. Click the + symbol next to **IDE ATA/ATAPI controllers**, as shown in Figure 7-5.

6. Double-click **Primary IDE Channel**.

7. Click the **Advanced Settings** tab.

8. Under **Device 0**, ensure the **Transfer Mode** is set to **DMA if available**, as shown in Figure 7-6.

9. Under **Device 1**, ensure the **Transfer Mode** is set to **DMA if available** (see Figure 7-6).

10. Click **OK**.

11. Double-click **Secondary IDE Channel**.

12. Repeat steps 7 through 10.

13. Close all open windows.

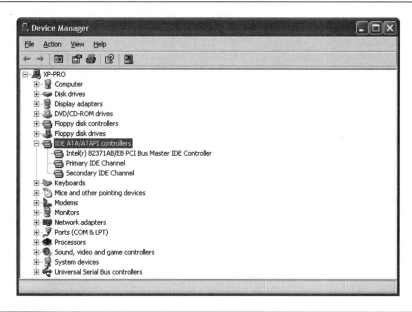

**FIGURE 7-5** Windows XP Device Manager

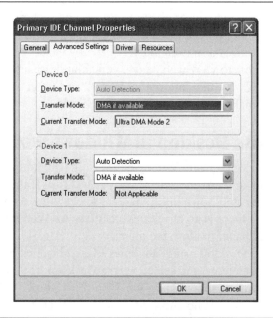

**FIGURE 7-6** Checking the DMA setting in Windows XP

NOTE *For all versions of Windows, if you wish to verify that your settings have taken effect, simply repeat the instructions here for your version of Windows, and the current settings will be displayed. If everything looks as it should, click Cancel and close the windows. If the setting changed itself back, you may have incompatible hardware, or there may be a device driver issue or other reason your hardware cannot use DMA mode.*

# Active Desktop

Active Desktop is a Windows feature that allows you to make your desktop act like your own personal web page. You can display pieces of your favorite web sites directly on your desktop and keep them up-to-date automatically. Although this might sound like a great idea, it consumes quite a bit of resources and can cause poor PC performance. On many computers, enabling this setting not only results in an overall decrease in system performance, but also causes an increase in the length of time it takes your computer to start.

Most people that have Active Desktop enabled don't even realize it; no web sites are displayed on their desktop, nor does their desktop appear any different than usual. However, the resources Active Desktop consumes are still being used, regardless of how the Active Desktop is configured.

For users of Windows 98/Me, when your computer is first turned on, you may see your desktop wallpaper appear, then disappear, and then reappear before the boot process is complete. If your desktop wallpaper vanishes during boot, this is a sure sign that Active Desktop is enabled.

It is my opinion that to view web pages, you should use a program designed for such a task (a web browser like Internet Explorer), and let your desktop just be a desktop. To do this, make sure Active Desktop is disabled.

## Disabling Active Desktop in Windows 98/Me

To disable Active Desktop using Windows 98, right-click any empty area of your desktop (not on an icon) and select **Active Desktop**. If there is a check next to **View As Web Page**, as shown in Figure 7-7, select **View As Web Page** and click to uncheck it. If there is no check next to **View As Web Page**, simply click anywhere on the wallpaper to close the menu.

To disable Active Desktop using Windows Me, right-click any empty area of your desktop (not on an icon) and select **Active Desktop**. If there is a check next to **Show Web Content**, as shown in Figure 7-8, select **Show Web Content** and click to uncheck it. If there is no check next to **Show Web Content**, simply click anywhere on the wallpaper to close the menu.

| FIGURE 7-7 | Active Desktop enabled on Windows 98 |

## Disabling Active Desktop in Windows XP

To disable Active Desktop in Windows XP, follow these steps:

1. Click **Start**, click **Control Panel**, and double-click the **Display** icon.

2. Click the tab labeled **Desktop** and click the **Customize Desktop...** button.

3. Click the tab labeled **Web**.

4. Ensure there is no check next to **My Current Home Page** (or next to any other items in this dialog box), as shown in Figure 7-9. If any items are selected, uncheck them.

| FIGURE 7-8 | Active Desktop enabled on Windows Me |

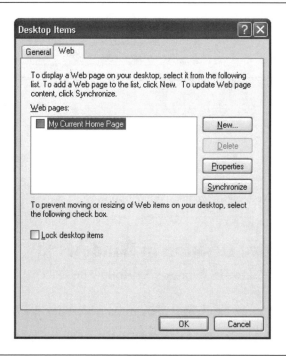

**FIGURE 7-9**   Active Desktop disabled in Windows XP

**5.** Click **OK**.

**6.** Click **OK**, and then close the Control Panel.

# Unnecessary Animations

Cute mouse pointers and other visual effects can tax your computer. If you want your computer to run at its top speed, don't burden it with needless visual entertainment that obstructs its ability to be as productive as possible.

Cute mouse pointers that dance about may be amusing, but unless you have a powerful system with lots of memory, do you really want to burden your computer and wait longer for your computer to complete tasks in exchange?

If you're running Windows 98 or Me, you have a Desktop Themes option. Activating this option also adds visual enhancements at the cost of performance.

## Disabling Unnecessary Animations in Windows 98/Me

To disable unnecessary animations in Windows 98/Me, follow these steps:

1. Click **Start**, click **Settings**, and then click **Control Panel**.

2. Double-click the **Display** icon.

3. Click the tab labeled **Effects** and uncheck all items, except for **Show icons using all possible colors**, as shown in Figure 7-10.

4. Click **OK**.

5. Back at the Control Panel, double-click the **Desktop Themes** icon.

6. At the top of this window is a drop-down menu showing your current desktop theme. Click the down-arrow to display all of the installed themes, scroll down, and select **Windows Default**. Also, ensure that all of the options listed under Settings contain check marks. Your window should look like the one shown in Figure 7-11.

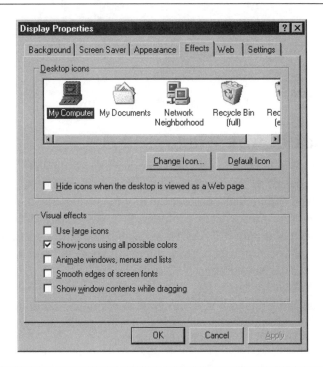

| FIGURE 7-10 | Windows 98 Display Effects properties |

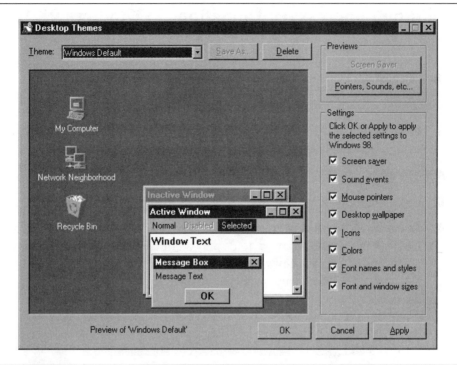

**FIGURE 7-11**   Desktop Themes settings in Windows 98

**7.** Click **OK**, and then close any remaining windows.

## Using Tweak UI with Windows 98/Me

Windows 98 and Windows Me users have another tool available to them
that Microsoft provides as an unsupported download only. This means that
although Microsoft technicians consider the tool to be valuable, they have no
intention of helping you resolve any problems that may result from installing
and using it. This tool is called Tweak UI and can be downloaded from this
Uniform Resource Locator (URL): www.microsoft.com/ntworkstation/
downloads/PowerToys/Networking/ NTTweakUI.asp.

The web page that appears offers full instructions on how to obtain and install
Tweak UI. When using this tool, it's important that you use caution when making
changes. As a general rule, if you obey the following guidelines, you should be
safe playing with all of the options Tweak UI offers.

- Do not change the **First icon on desktop** from **My Documents** (located at bottom of window).

- Do not uncheck **Search Results** on the **Desktop** tab.

- Do not uncheck (to hide) the **Tweak UI icon** on the **Control Panel** tab.

- Do not uncheck **Show Control Panel on Start Menu Settings** on the **IE** (Internet Explorer) tab.

- Do not uncheck **Shell enhancements** on the **IE** tab.

After you install Tweak UI, you'll have a new icon in your **Control Panel** labeled **Tweak UI**. Double-click it to start Tweak UI. From there, you can disable many of the unnecessary Windows animations that are otherwise unavailable for adjustment without this tool. You'll find these settings under the **General** tab, as shown in Figure 7-12.

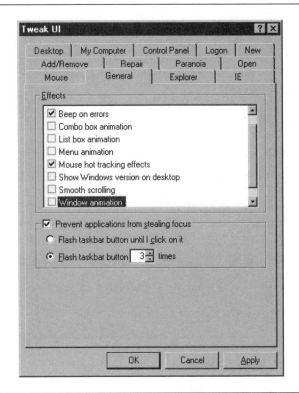

**FIGURE 7-12**    Disable unnecessary animations using the General tab of Tweak UI.

## Disabling Unnecessary Animations in Windows XP

With Windows XP, you can balance the visual effects against system performance by turning off all visual effects, letting your system decide which to use, or picking and choosing which effects to turn on or off. To disable unnecessary animations in Windows XP, follow these steps:

1.  Click **Start**, click **Control Panel**, and then double-click the **System** icon.

2.  Click the **Advanced** tab.

3.  Under the **Performance** section, click **Settings**. The **Performance Options** dialog box appears, as shown in Figure 7-13.

4.  The default setting is to allow Windows to determine which visual effects to turn on and off. To turn off all effects, choose **Adjust for best performance**. To use all visual effects, choose **Adjust for best appearance**. To turn on

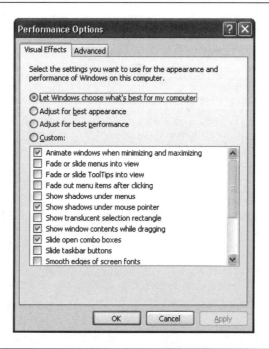

**FIGURE 7-13**    Performance Options dialog box in Windows XP

and off individual effects, choose **Custom**, and then check the effects you want to use and uncheck the ones you don't want to use.

5. Click **OK**.

6. Click **OK**, and then close any remaining windows.

# Fonts

Excess fonts not only hog system resources, but too many of them can actually cause your computer to crash! By default, Windows includes more than 50 fonts. Many people choose to install numerous additional fonts on their computers.

*[handwritten note: system fonts are in "red"]*

## How Many Fonts Are Too Many?

You can install a maximum of approximately 1,000 TrueType fonts in Microsoft Windows 98 and Windows Me. The exact number of TrueType fonts you can install varies, depending on the length of the TrueType font name and filenames. However, you will experience a decline in system performance much earlier than when you hit the maximum number of installed fonts allowed. Furthermore, Windows 98 and Windows Me will not tell you when you have reached the limit of installed fonts. In fact, those systems will even continue to let you think you are adding fonts to your system when you actually are not.

After you reach the maximum limit of installed fonts in Windows, you (or an installation program) can keep adding fonts to the Windows Fonts folder. The fonts will appear to be installed because they are in the folder, but they may not appear in the Font menu of your software. The fonts are unusable because you have exceeded your system's limit. When this occurs, you will find that as you delete fonts, the number of installed fonts that is indicated in the status bar when viewing the Windows Fonts folder does not change. This is because as you delete fonts, those extra, unusable fonts are moving up and becoming usable again. When you finally see this number in the status bar begin to decrease, you know you are making progress.

My recommendation is to keep under 450 fonts installed at any given time. Doing so will allow your system and software to start faster and run much smoother.

> **NOTE** *Windows XP users can add as many fonts as their hard disk can hold. However, while Windows XP won't crash as a result of too many installed fonts, it will still hinder the performance of the computer.*

## Taking Control of Your Fonts

To decrease the number of fonts on your computer, you can delete them, as follows:

1. Windows 98/Me users, click **Start**, click **Settings**, and then click **Control Panel**. Windows XP users, click **Start** and click **Control Panel**.

2. Double-click the **Fonts** icon.

3. To see what a font looks like, double-click its icon.

4. You can delete a font by right-clicking it and selecting **Delete**.

 *Do not delete Windows system fonts, which have the extension .fon instead of .ttf. The icon for a system font will have a red A, rather than a gray-blue TT. Also, some applications require specific fonts, such as Arial or Times New Roman, so you should keep them as well.*

If you use a lot of fonts, you may find font-management software beneficial, because it allows you to easily maintain control of your fonts. An excellent font-management utility called MyFonts is available for free from www.mytools.com. MyFonts lets you view and preview both installed and uninstalled fonts. You can install and uninstall fonts individually or in groups. You can also print professional-quality specimen sheets, in black and white or in full color, and you can compare fonts. MyFonts even includes a monitoring tool that checks to see if your font system has become unstable, as well as a counter to show you how many fonts you currently have installed.

# Windows Swap File

When Windows runs out of physical memory (random access memory, or RAM), it creates *virtual memory* by placing a file on your hard disk called a *swap file* (also commonly called a *paging file*). It's called a swap file because the operating system swaps data between it and main memory (RAM). Because RAM is purely *solid-state* (it has no moving parts), it can communicate with the rest of the system much faster than your hard disk, which has rotating platters and heads, similar to a record player and needle or a CD player and laser.

## How Does Swapping Work?

The hard disk was originally designed to be a storage area for your data and programs. Since RAM requires electricity to function, all of its contents are lost forever once you turn the computer off. The hard disk uses magnetism to store data, similar to how a videotape uses magnetism to store movies or an audio cassette uses magnetism to store music. If you were to run out of RAM while running a program (this typically occurs while using memory-intensive programs like image-editing software), the computer would ordinarily crash. However, Microsoft introduced an automated swap file, starting with Windows 95, which allows it to take the overflow of data and place it temporarily on the hard disk. While this results in slower system performance when swapping occurs, it sure beats a complete system crash!

In Chapter 1, you learned that it was important that you had at least ten percent of your hard disk available. Now you have a better understanding why. If Windows runs out of RAM, and then while moving excess data to the hard disk, runs out of space on the hard disk, you will encounter what is commonly referred to as a Blue Screen of Death (BSOD). Once this happens, all work not previously saved is lost, and the computer must be restarted. The computer will also need to check for data errors on the hard disk, because any files that were in an open state when the computer crashed may have been irreparably damaged.

When the computer reaches the end of the swap file, it behaves no differently than it would if your hard disk were full. The result is an unexpected crash, losing all of your work, and needing to reboot to get things going again. There is also the risk of permanently lost data.

## Swap File Misconceptions

There is much false information about how to configure a Windows swap file. One of the most common misconceptions is that you should set your swap file's maximum size to 2.5 times the amount of RAM you have installed in your system. For example, if you have 128MB of RAM installed in your computer, the proponents of this idea would have you set your swap file maximum size to 320MB. The problem with this logic is quite simple, yet even many seasoned technicians don't comprehend it. The more RAM you have, the less need you have for a swap file. This formula works in the exact opposite direction. For example, if you have 32MB of RAM, your need for a swap file will be greater than that of someone who has 128MB of RAM. Remember, a swap file is crucial to have once you fill up your physical memory (RAM). Yet, with 32MB of RAM, setting your swap file to a maximum of 2.5 times your RAM would result in a tiny maximum swap file size of just 80MB.

Other people monitor their swap file usage and then set their minimum and maximum swap file size based on an average of the maximum size the computer has reported using in the last week or two. Because a swap file shrinks and grows, and because the hard disk is one of the slowest components of your system, setting the minimum and maximum size of their swap file to the same size will ensure that the swap file will never shrink or grow. This also prevents fragmentation from occurring and decreases the hard disk's work during the shrinking and growing process. This works great for a few weeks, and sometimes months— if you are a robot and always use your computer the same way every day. But sooner or later, you will install a new piece of software or hardware, update an existing piece of software, or use the computer in a way you haven't used it before (perhaps you purchased a new scanner or digital camera and are now editing large, detailed images). Now, your data suddenly exceeds the maximum swap file size, resulting in an unexpected system crash.

This can be one of the most difficult problems to diagnose, because most people will have long since forgotten they set their minimum and maximum swap file size. They will try all sorts of misdirected techniques and advice from friends and technical support representatives to attempt to remedy the problem. Sooner or later, in many cases, they'll give up and just reinstall Windows, and everything will work again. Then they'll conclude it was a Windows problem all along and curse Microsoft, learning nothing in the process and never realizing it was their own undoing months before, all in the name of "performance."

NOTE    *Have you ever witnessed your computer making noise, as if it were very busy, when you're not even using it? Although there can be numerous reasons for this behavior, it is commonly caused by Windows during its automatic resizing of the swap file. Windows realizes you no longer need this large area of hard disk space that you were previously using, so it shrinks the swap file down to a minimal size.*

## Configuring Your Windows Swap File in Windows 98/Me

Because of improvements in swap file maintenance and control with Windows XP, manual swap file configuration is necessary for Windows 98 and Windows Me users only. Windows XP users do not need to make any changes and can safely skip this section.

In the following steps, we're going to configure the minimum swap file size only. By setting the minimum swap file size to 300MB and leaving the maximum swap file size alone, you allow the swap file to grow if necessary. This will also ensure that your swap file will never shrink below 300MB (so you won't hear your hard disk thrashing about as often when you are not doing anything on the computer), and that 300MB of your hard disk will always be reserved for Windows. This way, if you fill up your hard disk entirely, there is a good chance Windows will continue to run without running out of virtual memory.

**CAUTION** *Once you change the swap file size setting, your computer will require a reboot. Make sure all windows and/or applications are closed before starting this procedure.*

1. Click **Start**, click **Settings**, and then click **Control Panel**.

2. Double-click the **System** icon.

3. Click the tab labeled **Performance**.

4. Click the **Virtual Memory** button, located in the lower-right side of the dialog box, as shown in Figure 7-14.

5. Select **Let me specify my own virtual memory settings**, as shown in Figure 7-15.

6. In the text box next to **Minimum**, type **300** (see Figure 7-15).

**NOTE** *Do not alter the amount shown as **Maximum**. This number will be the same as the amount of free space available on your hard disk. If you see a negative number displayed here, there is no need to worry; simply ignore it. Microsoft never planned the math used in this setting to include hard disks that are of the massive sizes that are available today. If seeing this negative number causes you distress, a fix is available from Microsoft. Visit http://support.microsoft.com/?kbid=272620 for details on how to obtain the fix.*

7. Click **OK**.

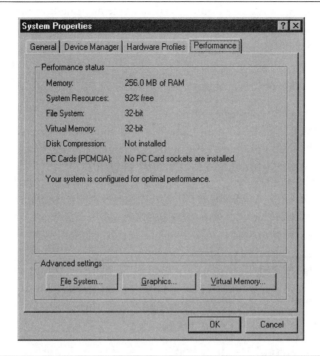

**FIGURE 7-14**    The Performance tab of the System Properties dialog box

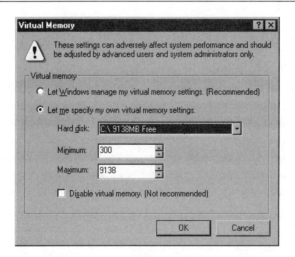

**FIGURE 7-15**    Windows 98 virtual memory settings

8. A warning message will appear, indicating that you are no longer allowing Windows to fully control the virtual memory/swap file, as shown in Figure 7-16. Click **Yes**.

9. Click **Close**.

10. Click **Yes** when asked if you want to restart your computer

11. To verify that your settings took effect, repeat steps 1 through 4. In Windows 98, the dialog box should show a minimum swap file size of 300, grayed out, and the maximum should read **No maximum**, as shown in Figure 7-17. Windows 98 users should also be aware that any time you view this window, the computer automatically defaults to selecting **Let Windows manage my virtual memory settings. (Recommended)**. This behavior is by design and is nothing to worry about as long as you do not click the **OK** button. In Windows Me, the dialog box should appear exactly as you set it. (If your settings did not take effect, you are having other difficulties with your computer.)

12. Click **Cancel,** and then click **Cancel** again.

13. Close any remaining windows.

## Summary

You should have noticed an increase in your computer's speed and reliability after following the suggestions in this chapter. You also understand how not using DMA mode, enabling Active Desktop, unnecessary animations, too many fonts, and improperly sized swap files can hinder your system's performance. Soon, you'll

FIGURE 7-16    Windows 98 warning message that appears after making changes to the swap file

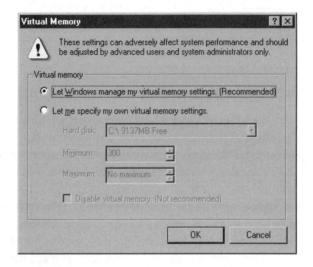

**FIGURE 7-17**   Windows 98 custom virtual memory settings in effect

feel the urge to correct friends, family members, and coworkers about their misconceptions of PC performance. You're taking on the qualities of a full-fledged computer nerd.

But don't order that pocket protector just yet! In the next chapter, you'll learn even more in-depth ways of how to enhance your Windows performance.

# Part III

## Optimize Windows Performance

# Chapter 8

# More Windows
# Performance Tips

Your Windows operating system is doing the best it can to handle all of the software demands that you have placed on it over the course of ownership. The more you demand of it, the slower it appears to run. On the other hand, if you instruct Windows to do less, it can give more of its attention to fewer tasks and complete those tasks faster.

As you purchase software and hardware, you add to the burden of your operating system. Some of this burden can be safely removed without affecting the added software or hardware.

Software and hardware manufacturers tend to be selfish when it comes to designing their products. They want you to have the best experience possible with their product and will produce software that preloads and is always ready when you need it. The idea here is that the program will start faster. As a result, Windows slows down each time another task is added to its startup routine. Popular programs such as Microsoft Office, Microsoft Works, and Intuit's Quicken place files in your startup routine, causing your Windows operating system to run slower and take longer to start up. All of the items these programs place in your Startup folder can be safely removed without any noticeable difference.

In this chapter, you'll discover how you can improve Windows performance by removing unnecessary software and disabling unnecessary programs from startup. And if you're a Windows XP user, you'll find some other tips for optimizing your computer's performance.

# Unnecessary Software and System Resources

The first step is to remove any software from your computer that you're not using. It's quite common to find items that were installed over the Internet without your knowledge or as part of another piece of software that you installed earlier. Many times, computer manufacturers load your computer with demonstration versions of software, as well as other items that are not only taking up your hard disk space, but also placing additional workload on your Windows operating system.

## Removing Unnecessary Software

To locate and remove unnecessary software from your computer, follow these steps:

1. For Windows 98/Me users, click **Start**, click **Settings**, and then click **Control Panel.** For Windows XP users, click **Start** and click **Control Panel.**

2. Double-click the **Add/Remove Programs** icon.

3. In the list that appears, look for software that you do not use. You may see files such as SaveNow, New.net, Gator, Precision Time and/or Xupitor in your list of installed programs. These are programs that promote advertising and run in the background without your knowledge, and they can be safely uninstalled.

> **NOTE**  *Be cautious when you are uninstalling programs. If you see software listed that you do not recognize, it's best to leave it alone, rather than learn what it is after you've removed it.*

4. To uninstall a program, simply click it to select it, and then click the **Remove** button. If you see a dialog box asking if it is okay to remove a possible shared file, play it safe and click **No**.

> **NOTE**  *Some programs may require you to restart your computer to complete the uninstall process. If this request is made, allow your computer to restart, and then continue removing other unwanted software, until you have gone through the entire list.*

## Checking System Resources (for Windows 98/Me Users)

One of your goals is to reduce the amount of system resources consumed by unnecessary software so that more resources are available to Windows and the software applications that are beneficial to you. Windows 98 and Windows Me have an inherent limitation in the way they were designed. There are a finite amount of system resources available to these operating systems, and once you exceed this limitation, the computer will crash.

Many people (including many computer technicians) believe that you can increase system resources by adding more RAM to a system or increasing the size of its hard disk. This misconception stems from a common misunderstanding of exactly what system resources are and how Windows uses them. If, for example, you open 30 programs at the same time, there is a good chance your computer will run out of resources and crash. No amount of RAM or hard disk space will change this. It's inherent to how Windows works, and there is no known fix for it (other than to not run so many programs simultaneously or to upgrade to Windows XP).

> **NOTE**  *To learn more about the difference between system memory (RAM) and resources, visit http://aumha.org/win4/a/resource.htm.*

To determine the amount of system resources you currently have available (for Windows 98/Me users only), follow these steps:

1. Click **Start**, click **Settings**, and then click **Control Panel**.

2. Double-click the **System** icon.

3. Click the **Performance** tab. The window that appears should be similar to Figure 8-1 and will display the current percentage of system resources currently available to your PC.

NOTE   *While viewing your system resources, check that your **File System** and **Virtual Memory** are showing they are in **32-bit** mode. A computer running in 16-bit mode may run just fine; however, it is not running as efficiently or reliably as it could be. This is not a critical error to fix, but if you ever have a professional look at your PC for other reasons, you should ask the technician about repairing this for you, too.*

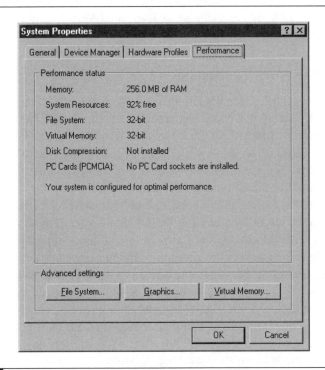

**FIGURE 8-1**   System resources reported in Windows 98/Me

**4.** When you are finished viewing your available system resources, click the **Cancel** button.

After removing items from startup, as described in the next section, be sure to check your system resources again to see how much of a difference you made. Always try to keep system resources above 30 percent if possible.

## Disabling Unnecessary Programs from Startup

Windows juggles each program that you load. The more programs you have running on your computer at once, the more likely it is that your computer will either run slowly or even crash. Just as it would be easier to juggle three balls than to juggle nine, it's easier for Windows to load fewer programs on startup.

Although Windows XP users don't need to worry about system resources, they can still benefit from disabling unnecessary programs from startup. This will allow the computer to start up faster.

Microsoft introduced a diagnostic utility called MSCONFIG with Windows 98 and has included it with Windows Me and Windows XP as well. Although this utility was designed to make it easier to troubleshoot computer problems, it can also be used to prevent numerous hidden programs from starting each time you boot your computer. Some of these hidden programs are essential, but you most likely have many that are not necessary. Turning off some of these hidden programs can significantly increase your computer's performance and reliability by freeing valuable system resources.

When you run MSCONFIG, you will see a list of the items your computer loads when it starts up. Depending on what software and hardware are installed on your system, which items are needed or can be removed will vary. Obviously, you don't want to disable your antivirus or firewall software from starting when Windows starts. Figure 8-2 shows the items a fresh installation of Windows 98 loads for itself. Figure 8-3 shows the items a fresh installation of Windows Me loads for itself. Windows XP loads nothing by default. Use this as a partial guide of knowing what to leave alone.

If you are uncertain what an item is, you can visit http://ww2.whidbey.net/djdenham/Uncheck.htm for an explanation of many startup items to help you decide if it is safe to disable the item from Windows startup. Alternatively, you can visit http://www.pacs-portal.co.uk/startup_pages/startup_full.htm, or you can use the search functions of Google at www.google.com to look up a specific item.

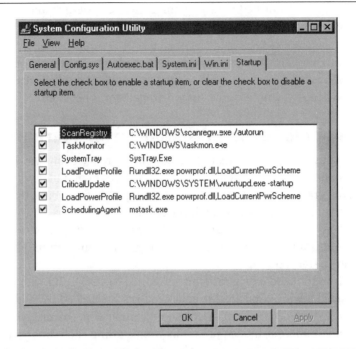

**FIGURE 8-2** Windows 98 default startup files

Here is how to use the MSCONFIG utility to disable some of the unnecessary programs that automatically load on startup:

1. Click **Start**, click **Run**, type **MSCONFIG**, and click **OK**.

2. Click the tab labeled **Startup.** The list that appears shows every item that your computer must load and run each time you start your computer. Some of these files are essential to the proper operation of Windows, but some of these files can be safely unchecked so they do not run at startup.

3. After you have unchecked the items you feel are unnecessary, click **OK**. Windows will then need to restart. Now, it should restart faster, depending on how many items you deselected.

4. Windows Me and XP users will be alerted with a message once Windows is restarted, letting you know that you have chosen to not load all items at startup, as shown in Figure 8-4. Simply place a check in the box next to

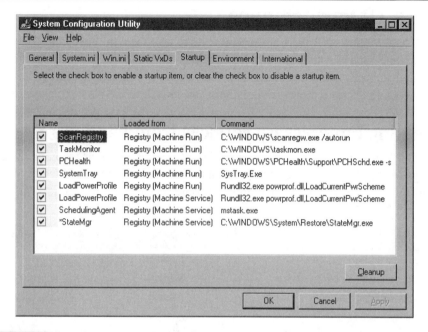

FIGURE 8-3   Windows Me default startup files

**Don't show this dialog again** and click **OK** to prevent this message from popping up in the future. If you make changes using MSCONFIG in the future, it will be necessary to repeat this process.

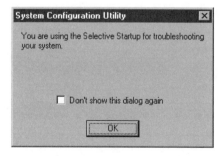

**FIGURE 8-4**   Warning message that appears in Windows Me after deselecting items from MSCONFIG and restarting the computer

# Windows XP Performance

If you have Windows XP, there are several ways that you can improve your computer's performance. One way to improve performance with Windows XP is to disable any unneeded services that are running. Another way is to turn off its error reporting and automatic restart features. Finally, you can switch to the NTFS file system.

## Disabling Unnecessary Services from Windows XP

Table 8-1 lists common services found in Windows XP and their recommended settings for most people. Your computer may not have all of these listed services installed or available and also may include some services not in this list.

| Service | Recommended Setting |
| --- | --- |
| Alerter | Disabled |
| Application Layer Gateway Service | Manual |
| Application Management | Manual |
| Automatic Updates | Automatic |
| Background Intelligent Transfer Service | Disabled |
| ClipBook | Disabled |
| COM+ Event System | Manual |
| COM+ System Application | Manual |
| Computer Browser | Automatic |
| Cryptographic Services | Automatic |
| DHCP Client | Automatic |
| Distributed Link Tracking Client | Manual |
| Distributed Transaction Coordinator | Manual |
| DNS Client | Automatic |
| Error Reporting Service | Disabled |
| Event Log | Automatic |
| Fast User Switching Capability | Manual |
| Fax | Automatic |
| Help and Support | Automatic |
| Human Interface Device Access | Disabled |
| IMAPI CD-Burning COM Service | Automatic |

**TABLE 8-1**  Windows XP Services and Recommended Settings

| Service | Recommended Setting |
| --- | --- |
| Indexing Service | Disabled |
| Internet Connection Firewall (ICF)/Internet Connection Sharing (ICS) | Automatic |
| IPSec Services | Disabled |
| Logical Disk Manager | Manual |
| Logical Disk Manager Administrative Service | Manual |
| Machine Debug Manager | Disabled |
| Messenger | Disabled |
| MS Software Shadow Copy Provider | Manual |
| Net Logon | Automatic |
| NetMeeting Remote Desktop Sharing | Disabled |
| Network Connections | Manual |
| Network DDE | Disabled |
| Network DDE DSDM | Disabled |
| Network Location Awareness (NLA) | Manual |
| NT LM Security Support Provider | Manual |
| Performance Logs and Alerts | Disabled |
| Plug and Play | Automatic |
| Portable Media Serial Number Service | Disabled |
| Print Spooler | Automatic |
| Protected Storage | Automatic |
| QoS RSVP | Disabled |
| Remote Access Auto Connection Manager | Manual |
| Remote Access Connection Manager | Manual |
| Remote Desktop Help Session Manager | Disabled |
| Remote Procedure Call (RPC) | Automatic |
| Remote Procedure Call (RPC) Locator | Manual |
| Remote Registry | Disabled |
| Removable Storage | Manual |
| Routing and Remote Access | Disabled |
| Secondary Logon | Disabled |
| Security Accounts Manager | Automatic |
| Server | Automatic |

**TABLE 8-1**    Windows XP Services and Recommended Settings *(continued)*

| Service | Recommended Setting |
| --- | --- |
| Shell Hardware Detection | Automatic |
| Smart Card | Disabled |
| Smart Card Helper | Disabled |
| SSDP Discovery Service | Disabled |
| System Event Notification | Automatic |
| System Restore Service | Automatic |
| Task Scheduler | Automatic |
| TCP/IP NetBIOS Helper | Automatic |
| Telephony | Manual |
| Telnet | Disabled |
| Terminal Services | Manual |
| Themes | Automatic |
| Uninterruptible Power Supply | Disabled |
| Universal Plug and Play Device Host | Disabled |
| Upload Manager | Disabled |
| Volume Shadow Copy | Manual |
| WebClient | Disabled |
| Windows Audio | Automatic |
| Windows Image Acquisition (WIA) | Automatic |
| Windows Installer | Manual |
| Windows Management Instrumentation | Automatic |
| Windows Management Instrumentation Driver Extensions | Manual |
| Windows Time | Automatic |
| Wireless Zero Configuration | Automatic |
| WMI Performance Adapter | Disabled |
| Workstation | Automatic |

**TABLE 8-1**    Windows XP Services and Recommended Settings *(continued)*

If any of these services are active but not used on your computer, you can disable them. For example, if you are the only user of your computer and you do not have an Uninterruptible Power Supply (UPS)—a battery backup device that supplies your PC with power in case of a power failure—you can safely disable the Fast User Switching Capability and Uninterruptible Power Supply services.

TIP

*More information on specific services configurations and optimizations has been compiled and made available for free on the Internet from a gentleman who goes by the name Black Viper. His web page is very informative and contains recommended service settings for Windows XP, as well as other helpful computer-related information. His web site is located at www.blackviper.com.*

To view and disable services in Windows XP, follow these steps:

1. Click **Start** and click **Control Panel**.

2. Double-click **Administrative Tools**.

3. Double-click **Services**.

4. Each service is listed alphabetically on the right side of your screen. Click the name of a service to display a description of what that service is used for.

5. Double-click the name of the service to open a dialog box with a drop-down list that offers the options **Automatic**, **Manual**, or **Disabled**. This allows you to control when or if that service should start.

6. Choose the appropriate service setting. Refer to Table 8-1 for a list of common services and recommended settings. (Disregard services not included in Table 8-1.) Pay attention to the description of the service. Regardless of the recommendation in Table 8-1, if you think you need any particular service, leave that service set to **Automatic**. If your computer is already set to the setting recommended here, simply click the **Cancel** button and move onto the next service.

7. After making a change to a service, click **OK**, and then move onto the next one.

## Turning Off Error Reporting and Automatic Restart in Windows XP

By default, when Windows XP encounters an error, it shows a window asking if you want to send this information to Microsoft. Most people find this window to be an annoyance. In addition, if a critical error occurs, Windows XP is instructed to restart itself, which may not give you enough time to read the error message before the computer restarts. When a critical error occurs, it's best to reset the computer yourself once you've made a note of the exact error message.

To prevent Windows from restarting itself on critical errors and to prevent Windows from asking if you want to inform Microsoft every time a minor error occurs, follow these quick and simple steps:

1. Click **Start** and click **Control Panel**.

2. Double-click **System**.

3. Click the tab labeled **Advanced**.

4. Click the **Error Reporting** button at the bottom of the System Properties dialog box, as shown in Figure 8-5.

5. Select **Disable error reporting**. Place a check in the box next to **But notify me when critical errors occur**, as shown in Figure 8-6. Then click **OK**.

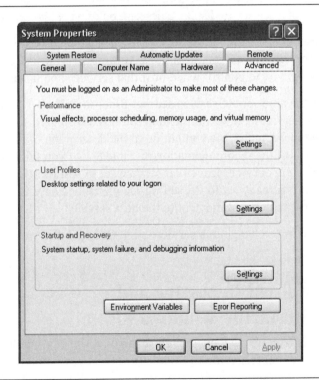

**FIGURE 8-5**   The System Properties dialog box in Windows XP

FIGURE 8-6    Disabling error reporting in Windows XP

**6.** In the System Properties dialog box, in the **Startup and Recovery** section, click the **Settings** button.

**7.** Uncheck the option to **Automatically restart**, as shown in Figure 8-7.

**8.** Click **OK,** and then click **OK** again.

## Using NTFS in Windows XP

The way in which an operating system organizes and keeps track of files on the hard disk is called a *file system*. Windows XP users will be using either a FAT32 or NTFS file system. (Windows 98/Me users will be using a file system called FAT16 or FAT32.)

To determine which file system your computer is using, double-click the **My Computer** icon located on your desktop and click **Local Disk (C:)**. The lower-left side of the window will display the details of the file system of the selected disk. See Figure 8-8 for an example.

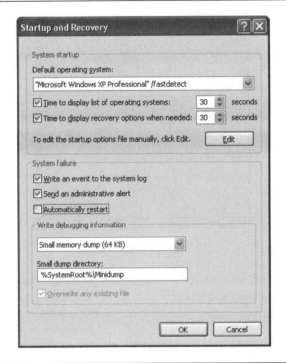

**FIGURE 8-7** Disabling automatic restart on critical errors in Windows XP

*C DRIVE PROPERTIES*

If you're running Windows XP and your hard disk is formatted as FAT32, use the following steps to convert it to the more robust, secure, and reliable NTFS file system:

**CAUTION** *Before following these steps, ensure that you have a backup copy of any important data on your computer. If you are uncertain of how to do this, bookmark this page and come back to it after reading how to back up your data in Chapter 9. Converting the file system will probably work flawlessly. However, a virus or power outage during the conversion process could result in damaging the data on the hard disk, even up to the point of necessitating a reinstallation of Windows. This process should not be taken lightly.*

1. Click **Start**, click **Run,** type **CMD,** and click **OK.**

2. Type **convert c: /fs:ntfs** and press the **Enter** key on your keyboard.

3. When the process is complete, type **EXIT** and press the **Enter** key on your keyboard.

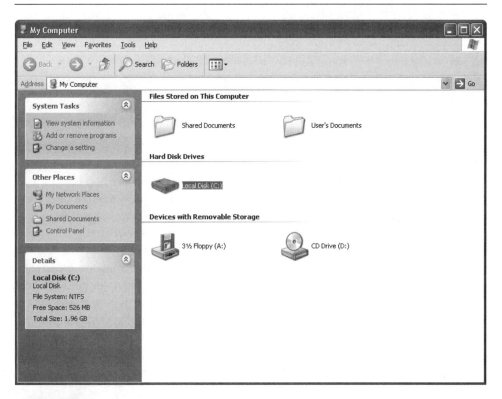

| FIGURE 8-8 | Details of the file system of the C: disk on a typical Windows XP computer |
|---|---|

## File System Facts

FAT is short for File Allocation Table. NTFS is short for New Technology File System. NTFS was first introduced with Windows NT, hence the name.

The NTFS file system is preferred for Windows XP users because it reduces the risk of data loss during a critical error or improper shutdown. It also adds file security to effectively keep out uninvited, prying eyes. NTFS also works better with larger hard disks. As hard disk size increases, so does the complexity of keeping track of all the data contained within the disk. NTFS handles this task much better and more reliably than FAT32.

By comparison, the FAT16 file system, which was included with DOS and the first edition of Windows 95, cannot format a disk larger then 2GB. That means that if you had a 20GB disk, you would need to separate it into ten 2GB pieces (this is called *partitioning*), and each 2GB piece would be assigned a drive letter. This would be very confusing and inconvenient.

## Summary

You now have a better understanding of what system resources are and how they relate to RAM than many computer technicians! You've removed some of the workload from your PC, which will enable it to run faster and more reliably. You've even learned a bit about file systems without being overwhelmed with technical details.

You've come a long way since Chapter 1, and you've tackled some progressively complicated computer issues each step of the way. In the next chapter, you'll learn whether it's best to turn off your PC or just leave it on, as well as how to use the Windows power settings and keep your computer running even if you have a power failure. You'll also learn how to make a backup copy of the data you have created, using some of the latest gadgets that make backing up your data easy.

Can you believe you're doing all of this on your own? And you thought this stuff was over your head!

# Chapter 9

# Safe Computing

E lectrical spikes, which typically occur when a storm is in your area, have cost many a PC owner a pretty penny in repairs. Not only are you inconvenienced by not having your PC while it is being repaired (and paying for this inconvenience), but in many cases, you permanently lose all of your data as well.

In this chapter, you'll learn how to protect your computer and your data from such disasters, as well as get answers to some commonly asked questions related to these issues.

# Leave the PC On or Turn It Off?

Many people are uncertain whether it is best to leave their PC on or to turn it off. Although there is no one definitive answer, generally speaking, it is best to turn off the PC if it is not going to be used for more than two hours.

Leaving a computer on means allowing all the fans to turn. When the fans turn, this circulates air through the system. As the air moves through the system, it brings dust with it. The dust settles on the inside of the computer and acts as an insulator, causing the system to run hotter. (When you put on a coat, you are insulating yourself.) Over time, the system will continue to run hotter and hotter. Also, if the fan bearings become contaminated with dust, the fans will start to vibrate and make noise. Fans are crucial in today's modern computers, which run very fast and very hot.

When a fan starts to fail, it is usually accompanied by a loud, vibrating noise. If you turn off a computer with a failing fan, it's quite possible the fan will not start again. While the computer is running, the grease in the fan is warm, and the fan rotates without much friction. But when the dust and grease cool down, they may form a kind of glue. Most modern computers won't allow the PC to turn on if the main processor fan has failed. However, not all PCs are guaranteed to check for this. It's very important that you get noisy fans replaced as soon as possible for this reason. If you have a fan that is sometimes noisy and other times quiet, ask yourself this question: Is it quiet because it got better or is it quiet because it stopped completely?

The computer's hard disk spins between 5,400 and 7,200 rotations per minute (RPM). Some high-end systems have hard disks that spin from 10,000 to 15,000 RPM! This motion creates friction. Friction creates heat. Heat causes excessive wear and tear. The cooler your computer runs, the faster it will run. It will also be less likely to have other heat-related errors.

CAUTION *Even though your monitor eats up more electricity than your computer, it still costs only pennies a day to run the monitor and computer all the time. You can tell Windows to put components such as your hard disk and monitor in to a low-power standby mode after a certain period of time elapses with no PC activity. This can help extend the life of the system, but it can also cause premature failure of the components if they are not staying in standby mode for any considerable length of time before "waking up."*

Proponents of leaving a computer on all the time use the logic that turning the computer on and off causes stress on the internal electronics. This is true. When does a light bulb usually burn out? This often happens when you first turn it on. This is because when electricity is moving through the filament inside the light bulb, it gets very hot, very fast. This causes the filament to expand. When the light bulb is turned off, the filament cools off and contracts. Constant expanding and contracting of a component will eventually lead it to failure—just like taking a piece of metal and bending it back and forth until it snaps into two pieces.

The problem with this logic is that most people will get rid of their computer years before this damage has occurred to the point of failure. Think of it this way: Do you leave your television on all the time? Most people will own the same television longer than they will own any computer.

Also, if you have a high-speed, always-on Internet connection and you leave your computer on all of the time, this can be an open invitation to bad guys to pound on your PC at night while you are sleeping.

Computers running Windows 98/Me will eventually run out of resources if they are left on and never restarted. This will result in a crash and will force you to restart the computer (also called *rebooting*). By shutting the system down at night, you can avoid this particular problem.

## Using Windows Power Settings for Desktop Computers

If you must leave your computer on for hours unattended, you should use the Windows power-saving settings to power off your monitor and hard disk. This will prevent wear and tear, as well as save electricity. Over time, you'll have a lower electric bill, maintain a healthier PC, and even benefit the environment!

Follow these steps to use Windows power settings:

1. Windows 98/Me users, click **Start**, click **Settings**, and then click **Control Panel**. Windows XP users, click **Start** and click **Control Panel.**

2. Double-click the icon labeled **Display**.

3. Click the **Screen Saver** tab.

4. Windows 98/Me users, click the **Settings…** button located in the lower-right corner. Windows XP users, click the **Power…** button located in the lower-right corner.

5. In the **Power schemes** section, select **Always On**.

6. For the **Turn off monitor** option, use a setting that works best for you. Many people choose **After 30 mins**.

7. For the **Turn off hard disks** option, use a setting that works best for you. Many people choose **After 1 hour**. An example of the Power Options Properties dialog box with these settings is shown in Figure 9-1.

8. Click **OK**, click **OK** again, and then close the Control Panel.

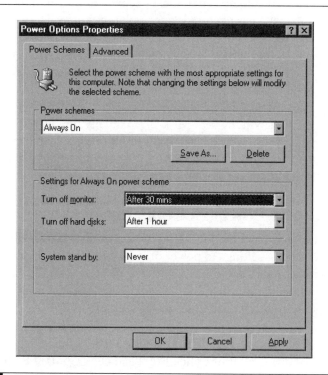

**FIGURE 9-1**    Setting Power Options in Windows 98/Me

NOTE
*I do not recommend using the **System stand by** or **Hibernation** mode for desktop computers. Many desktop computers do not awaken from System stand by or Hibernation modes because they were not designed to use them. These functions are beneficial to laptop owners only.*

9. Click the **Advanced** tab and make sure all the options available here are unchecked.

10. Windows XP users who are not using a laptop should click the **Hibernate** tab and uncheck **Enable hibernation**, as shown in Figure 9-2.

## Using Windows Power Settings for Laptop Computers

If you are using a laptop, your power options will look a little different than they do on a desktop computer. You have two sets of power options available: One when you are using your laptop's battery and one when your laptop is plugged into an electrical outlet, as shown in Figure 9-3.

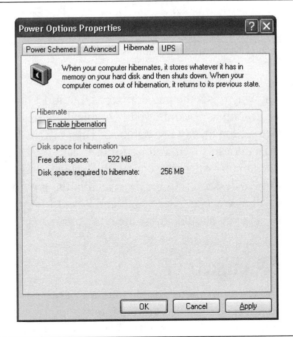

**FIGURE 9-2** Disable hibernation mode in Windows XP if this is not a laptop computer.

**FIGURE 9-3**   Laptop power settings in Windows XP

There is no wrong way to set the power options, but most laptop owners want their batteries to last as long as possible, so they typically adjust the settings in the **Running on batteries** section to very low numbers. This way, the laptop will conserve more battery power if it doesn't wait as long for user activity. Using the **Plugged in** section options, the laptop owner may choose to disable power settings altogether, or set them similar to the desktop settings described in the previous section.

Laptop owners will also see an Alarms tab and Power Meter tab. These options are self-explanatory, and you should adjust them to your own preferences.

# Do I Need a Screensaver?

Those cute screensavers can be more trouble than they are worth. Also be aware that many free screensavers available from the Internet are spyware.

Screensavers were a necessity years ago when computer monitors were prone to suffer from *burn-in*. Burn-in occurs when the same image is displayed unaltered for hours at a time, day after day. The phosphors in the monitor literally burn from being left on, leaving a shadow-like image of the display visible, even when the monitor is turned off. You may have noticed this at the airport on the monitors that display the airline arrival and departure times or on commercial arcade games that are several years old. Screensavers were used to constantly change the image on the monitor so that no burn-in could occur.

Think of how a magnifying glass works. If you hold it over an object in the sun at just the right angle, and do not move the magnifying glass, the object will get hotter and hotter and eventually melt or catch fire. If you constantly move the magnifying glass, the light doesn't stay on the object long enough to do any damage.

Most modern computer monitors have anti-burn-in technology built into them. Since screensavers consume resources, can cause conflicts, and offer nothing related to productivity in return, they are simply a waste of power. Using the power options in Windows to instruct your monitor to turn off (the monitor actually goes into a low-power standby mode and does not actually turn off), you are not only saving money and your screen from burn-in, but you are also not needlessly consuming resources from your PC.

If you insist on using a screensaver, configure your screensaver so that it comes on *before* you have instructed Windows to turn off the monitor. And be sure to still allow Windows to turn off the monitor after a certain period of time elapses. For example, many people have their screensaver come on if there is no activity on the computer for 10 minutes, and they instruct Windows to turn off their monitor if there is no activity for 30 minutes.

To select when you want the screensaver to activate, or to disable your screensaver completely, follow these steps:

1. Windows 98/Me users, click **Start**, click **Settings**, and then click **Control Panel**. Windows XP users, click **Start** and click **Control Panel**.

2. Double-click the icon labeled **Display**.

3. Click the **Screen Saver** tab. The dialog box that appears is self-explanatory. Click the different options here to become more familiar with them.

4. Click **OK** when you are finished, and then close the Control Panel.

# What's a UPS?

An Uninterruptible Power Supply (UPS) contains a rechargeable battery that provides power to your computer and monitor (and anything else you have plugged into it) if you experience a power failure while working on your computer.

## Microsoft Plus! Pack Screensavers

If you must use a screensaver, using one that is included with Windows will reduce the chances of incompatibility problems, which can commonly occur when using third-party screensavers.

Microsoft has released a Plus! Pack for Windows 98, Windows Me, and Windows XP that includes some spectacular screensavers and desktop themes. Note that the Plus! Pack installs only *unnecessary* software on the computer and is for entertainment purposes only.

One of the most impressive screensavers I have seen is included with the Microsoft Plus! Pack for Windows XP and is called Plus! Aquarium. Those who do not have the Plus! Pack can download a *demo* (short for demonstration) copy of this screensaver, called Marine Aquarium v.2.0 in the demo version, for free (and it's not spyware) from www.serenescreen.com. This demo will work on Windows 98, Windows Me, and Windows XP—provided that your computer and video card have enough power to run it. For more information about Microsoft's Plus! Pack for Windows XP, see www.microsoft.com/windows/plus/PlusHome.asp.

Most clock radios have a place to install a battery (or batteries) that keeps the time and the alarm setting, in case the power goes out while you're asleep. This ensures that when the power comes back on, your alarm clock will still wake you up, rather than just reset itself with the infamous blinking 12:00. This is a form of a UPS.

Some UPS units even filter the "dirty" power coming from your wall, allowing a cleaner power source to your computer and peripherals. These are called *continuous UPS* units. A UPS that provides power to your computer only when there is a power failure, spike, or sag in the voltage is referred to as a *standby UPS*. The standby UPS units are the most common, because they cost about half as much as continuous UPS units.

A UPS's main job is to buy you enough time so that you can save your work and shut down your computer properly when a power failure occurs. You should not continue to work on the computer during a power failure, or eventually the batteries on the UPS will drain completely. Then your computer will be improperly shut down and data may be lost, which defeats the purpose of having a UPS.

Also, a UPS that specifies that it can provide power to a computer and 15-inch monitor for 20 minutes means just that. If you have your printer, speakers, scanner, and 19-inch monitor plugged into the same UPS, it will drain the batteries that much faster.

NOTE

*A UPS should not be confused with a surge suppressor (sometimes called a surge protector or power strip). You may have your computer and peripherals plugged into a surge suppressor and believe you are protecting them from power surges and spikes. More than likely, the surge suppressor you have is little more than a convenient way to plug many devices in, since the electrical outlet in your wall has only two plugs available. Most surge suppressors sold for under $15 do little, if anything, to actually protect your computer or peripherals.*

Like a cordless phone or any other device that uses batteries, the UPS's batteries will eventually go bad (usually in two to three years). In most cases, the UPS batteries cannot be replaced, so you will need a new UPS unit. Also, because of the rechargeable batteries, it is illegal in most counties in the United States to dispose of UPSs along with your regular household garbage. They must be taken to a proper disposal/recycling facility. Most manufacturers of UPS units will provide, on request, a shipping label to a recycling service, so you can send the unit to a facility for proper disposal.

One of the largest UPS manufacturers is American Power Conversion Corp. (APC). This company sells units that will plug into your computer's USB port and will instruct the computer to power down automatically if the electricity does not come back on before the UPS unit's batteries run out of juice. To see this company's offerings, visit www.apcc.com.

If you're interested in learning more about UPS units and surge protectors, visit http://computer.howstuffworks.com/surge-protector.htm.

## What Is a USB Port?

If your computer is a Pentium II or higher, chances are it has at least one USB port. USB stands for Universal Serial Bus. It was designed because manufacturers were improperly using the computer's printer port (also called a parallel port) for hooking up scanners, Zip drives, and other devices that are clearly not printers. Many people had problems getting these devices to work, especially if they had more than one device plugged into the printer port. Since most computers have only one printer port, this meant that manufacturers of scanners and Zip drives had to provide an additional printer port on their device so people would have somewhere to plug in their printer.

Some people would plug their scanner into their computer's printer port, their Zip drive into the spare port on the back of the scanner, and their printer on the spare port of the Zip drive. Getting this configuration to work was a challenge, and even impossible in some cases.

The introduction of the USB port meant that all of the configuration issues could be avoided by implementing a new standard interface for computer peripherals. Using USB, you simply load the drivers for your USB device, and then plug your device into the USB port.

Another advantage to USB is that you can add and remove devices while the computer is on. This makes it very convenient if you have a USB device that you want to use only periodically, such as when transferring images from a digital camera or making backups.

Most older computers came with only two USB ports, usually located directly under the keyboard and mouse ports on the back of a computer. Newer computers include up to six USB ports, including one or two on the front of the computer. For example, you may want to plug in your digital camera to your computer to transfer the pictures. Rather than reach around the back of the computer trying to locate a USB port, you could simply plug it into the front of the PC for quick, easy access.

There are three kinds of USB. USB 1.0 and 1.1 transfer data at 12 megabits per second (Mbps). The newer USB 2.0 standard allows transfer speeds of 480 Mbps (about 40 times faster). You can plug in as many as 127 devices that can share the USB bandwidth. (The more devices you add, the slower each one will go if you're using them at the same time.) USB 2.0 is backward-compatible with USB 1.0 and 1.1; however, if you plug a USB 1.0 or 1.1 device into a USB 2.0 socket, every USB device (regardless of which USB version each device supports) will run at the slower 1.0 or 1.1 speed.

# Back Up Your Important Data!

A hard disk may fail without warning. One day it worked fine, and the next day it's dead (just like a light bulb). New viruses are written every day, and even a power outage while the computer is on can cause data loss, not to mention the possibility of theft or an accident. By taking a little time now to make a backup copy of your data, you're buying a little peace of mind. You will know that if something catastrophic happens to your hard disk, your data will be safe.

Many people don't know how to make a backup copy of data and simply think that they'll do it some other day. I guarantee that once you've lost all your data unexpectedly (and it will always be unexpectedly and usually at the worst possible time), you will learn how to make backups and back up your data religiously.

When many people think of making a backup, they believe that they must back up the entire hard disk. This is not only unnecessary and time-consuming, but it can be extremely challenging to recover such a backup. Since most backup devices need Windows to operate or to load software, that would mean you would need to reinstall Windows in order to restore your backup of Windows. Now, that doesn't make too much sense, does it?

Other people believe that copying data from one internal hard disk to another is a good backup system. Some people are under the false impression that creating a separate partition on their hard disk for their data is an effective backup. They couldn't be more wrong. Internal hard disks can fail at any time; they are prone to viruses, theft, fires, floods, or other disasters. The only backup worth making is one you can store away from the computer.

If your hard disk fails, it's enough of a hassle to need to reinstall and reconfigure Windows, your printer, scanner, email, and numerous other applications. As long as you have the original installation CDs, this is a mere annoyance. Now imagine you have no backup of all the data you created with those programs. Sure, your computer is up and running again, but what good is it without all the things you created? Digital pictures, music, genealogy, checkbook information, and so on—all lost forever. Yes, you could contract with a hard disk recovery service, but that can run in the thousands of dollars, and most people don't think their data is worth that much or can afford that service.

No special software is required to back up your data, and your data is all you should be concerned with backing up. Remember that you can reinstall programs, but you may never be able to re-create data exactly as it was before (and even if you could, do you really want to do that?).

There are numerous ways to back up your data: using floppy disks, Zip disks, CD-ROM and DVD-ROM recorders, tape drives, external hard disks, and USB thumb drives. Because floppy disks and tape drives are unreliable and slow, and CD-ROM and DVD recorders require special software to make CDs and DVDs, I'll explain how to back up your data to a Zip disk, an external hard disk, or a USB thumb drive.

NOTE *A Zip disk looks similar to a floppy disk in size and shape (only a little thicker) and can store 100MB, 250MB, or even up to 750MB of data, depending on which model you own. Zip disks require a Zip drive to be used, just as a floppy disk requires a floppy drive. A single 250MB Zip disk can store as much data as 173 floppy disks. To learn more about Zip drives, visit www.iomega.com.*

## Using a USB Thumb Drive

A USB thumb drive is a very small, solid-state (no moving parts; everything is electronic rather than mechanical) device that can quite commonly fit comfortably on a key chain. Manufacturers have unique names for these drives, but they are generically called *thumb drives*, or sometimes *flash drives*, because they store data using *flash memory*. Figure 9-4 shows an example of a USB thumb drive available from Trek 2000 International Ltd. (www.thumbdrive.com).

Flash memory is a type of electrically erasable programmable read-only memory (EEPROM) chip. For example, all digital cameras use flash memory to store the pictures they take.

Are your eyes glazing over yet? Don't worry! All you need to know is that these devices can store your data safely for up to 10 years, can withstand 1,000 g's of shock, are immune to magnetism (unlike floppies and Zip disks), can safely go through airport x-ray machines, and can take more abuse than any other kind of

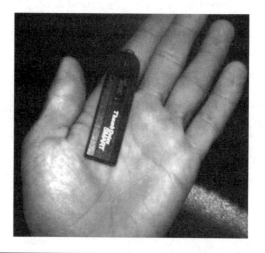

FIGURE 9-4    A USB thumb drive offered by Trek 2000 International Ltd.

consumer-based media. They are highly reliable and very durable, not to mention easy to use and configure, as well as inexpensive.

USB thumb drives come in a range of capacities and designs. Several manufacturers offer features for security and data privacy to differentiate their products from the competition. All USB thumb drives can be erased and overwritten thousands of times. Typical sizes available for USB thumb drives are 16MB, 32MB, 64MB, 128MB, 256MB, 512MB, 1GB, and 2GB.

> NOTE
>
> *GB is short for gigabyte and is equal to 1,000MB. MB is short for megabyte and is equal to 1,000 bytes. A byte is typically represented by one letter, number, space, or symbol.*

A floppy disk holds 1.44MB of data, is prone to data errors, and can be ruined if you get a magnetized screwdriver (or any other magnet) too close to it. The smallest USB thumb drive is equivalent to the data capacity of over 11 floppy disks, and it doesn't require a special drive to read it, unlike a floppy disk, CD-ROM, or Zip disk. All you need is any computer with a spare USB port and you're in business. Moving data from one computer to another and making backups couldn't be simpler.

## Backing Up Your Data

Ultimately, where you store your data is up to you. Microsoft products like to default to the My Documents folder. If you make it a point to store all of your pictures, music, and other data in the My Documents folder, all you'll need to do to back up your data is copy the My Documents folder from the C: drive (your hard disk) to your USB thumb drive, Zip drive, or external hard disk (provided they have enough free space available to hold your data).

> NOTE
>
> *Most data files are relatively small, but pictures and music can take up quite a bit of room. You may need to purchase additional storage media to back up pictures and music files, or use your CD or DVD recorder (if you have one) for long-term storage of pictures and music.*

Just about every program that you can run within Windows has a File menu at the top of the screen. You simply load your data into whatever program you are using, and then click **File**, choose **Save As...**, and select the **My Documents** folder as your destination storage area.

After all of your data is located in the My Documents folder, you can copy that directory to your backup device. Here are the steps for copying the My Documents folder:

1. Double-click the **My Computer** icon on your desktop and double-click your **C: drive**.

2. Windows XP users, double-click the folder labeled **Documents and Settings**, and then double-click the folder that should be labeled as your Windows logon name.

3. Double-click the **My Documents** folder in the list that appears.

4. Click **Edit** and click **Copy**. Then close the window.

5. Double-click **My Computer** and double-click the backup drive (the drive letter will vary from one PC to another, depending on the PC's unique configuration).

6. Click **Edit** and click **Paste**.

Your data is now being duplicated to your backup device. When the backup is completed, close any remaining windows. Then, be sure to put your backup copy in a safe place.

# Summary

In this chapter, you've learned how your PC uses power, the facts about screensavers, how to protect your computer from power outages and power spikes, and how to protect your precious data.

I can tell you're anxious to learn more because you've made it this far on your own and you're excited that you're actually "getting it."

The next chapter will be a little more challenging, but using what you've already learned, I'm sure you'll understand everything just as easily. In that chapter, you'll learn about upgrades. Which upgrades are worth the investment of money and time? You'll soon know the answer to this question and many more!

# Chapter 10

# Computer Upgrades

In this chapter, you'll learn about computer upgrades—which upgrades are worthwhile, which ones you can do yourself, and which ones are best left to professionals. Finally, it will help you determine when it's best to just start over with a new computer. You'll want to know all this before spending any money on a computer upgrade.

# Upgrading Your Operating System

If you're running Windows 98/Me and have been considering upgrading to Windows XP, you should know that the minimum requirements listed on the Windows XP box are not adequate for a pleasant experience with Windows XP. You should have at least an 800MHz computer with at least 256MB of RAM (memory). Although Windows XP will install on slower computers with less memory, it will operate exceptionally slowly. You'll be wondering why everyone talks about how great Windows XP is when Windows 98/Me ran much better for you.

Because the newer operating system is more stable and easier to use, its programming is more complex, and it demands more from your system.

When you are upgrading your operating system, keep in mind that installing one operating system on top of another is not recommended. Although Microsoft does offer upgrade versions of their operating systems for much less money than the cost of the full version, you can still use the upgrade version for a full installation, as long as you own a "qualifying product."

A fresh installation of the upgrade version of Windows XP Home edition will eventually stop and ask you to insert your Windows 98/Me CD. At this point, the installation temporarily stops, waiting for you to remove the Windows XP installation CD and insert your Windows 98/Me CD. After you have done that, click OK, and the Windows XP installation will verify that you own a qualifying product. Then it will instruct you to reinsert your Windows XP upgrade installation CD and continue with the install.

CAUTION    *Never upgrade an operating system over a preexisting operating system in an effort to fix a problem. In many cases, corrupted files are not replaced, and invalid information contained within the Windows registry will remain, causing the upgraded operating system to be extremely unreliable, if it even runs at all.*

# Adding Memory (RAM)

Adding RAM to your computer will help it run faster. However, tests show that Windows 98/Me does not efficiently use more than 192MB of RAM under common usage. What this means to you is that adding anything more than 192MB of RAM to a Windows 98 or Windows Me computer will not make much difference in how the computer performs, unless you use a specialized application that handles memory on its own, such as Adobe Photoshop.

Windows 98/Me can also actually have problems if more than 512MB of RAM is added. Ironically, Windows 98/Me systems with more than 512MB of RAM installed may start to experience out-of-memory errors. Although Microsoft has posted a workaround for this (http://support.microsoft.com/?kbid=253912), Windows won't efficiently use the memory anyway. I recommend that you save your money and not exceed 256MB of RAM on any Windows 98/Me computer.

Windows XP users will benefit from adding more memory without any caveats. Windows XP will use whatever you give it.

## Do I Need More RAM?

To determine how much RAM you have now, follow these steps:

1. Windows 98/Me users, click **Start**, click **Settings**, and click **Control Panel**. Windows XP users, click **Start** and click **Control Panel**.

2. Double-click the **System** icon.

3. In the **General** tab, the amount of RAM your computer has installed will be displayed in the lower-right part of the window, as well as what kind of central processing unit (CPU) is installed, as shown in Figure 10-1.

If you're running Windows XP and the amount of installed RAM is less than 512MB, consider upgrading your RAM. If you're running Windows 98/Me and the installed RAM is less than 192MB, I would recommend upgrading your memory only if you intend on keeping the system for another year. Adding RAM to an old system will not increase its value and only benefits you by making the machine a bit more responsive, reducing your wait times.

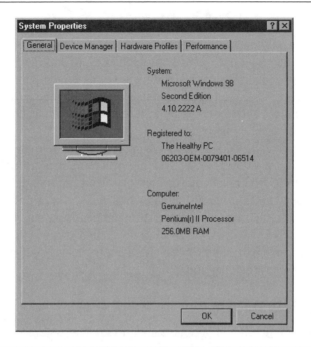

**FIGURE 10-1**    Windows 98 System Properties dialog box showing installed RAM

## CPU Speed

When viewing the General tab of the System Properties dialog box, Windows XP users will also see the actual speed of their processor. Note that it may be necessary to round the number, since Windows XP tends to be literal in its discovery process. For example, a 350MHz processor may be displayed as 348MHz. This is normal and nothing to be concerned about.

Windows 98/Me users will need to either watch for their CPU speed to be displayed when the computer is first turned on or download a utility that can present this information to you. SiSoftware Sandra (www.sisoftware.co.uk) works with all Windows operating systems and can give you such details (and much more) about your system.

# What Kind of RAM Is Compatible with My System?

If your computer has a Pentium III or Duron CPU, chances are your computer will require synchronous dynamic RAM (SD-RAM). However, except for the earliest models, most Celeron, Athlon, and Pentium IV CPUs require double data rate synchronous dynamic RAM (DDR-RAM). Also, to confuse things even further, some Pentium IV systems use Rambus dynamic RAM (RD-RAM).

Each type of RAM—SD-RAM, DDR-RAM, and RD-RAM—has its own unique design and will fit only into a computer specifically designed for it. RAM is relatively inexpensive and very easy to install. If your computer is manufactured by a major manufacturer such as Hewlett-Packard, Compaq, Dell, eMachines, Gateway, or IBM, you can look online to see what type of RAM your computer requires. Visit one of the major RAM manufacturers online at www.kingston.com or www.crucial.com and find the name and model of your PC in their database. If your computer was built by a local shop or by a friend, relative, or someone else, take your computer into a computer shop and have the shop's technician determine what kind of RAM your PC requires.

There is a limit to how much RAM can be installed, and this limit varies from one PC design to another. The web sites mentioned in the previous paragraph will tell you the maximum amount of RAM that your particular computer can handle. You may then choose to note this information and buy the RAM from a local retailer, or you might want to purchase it from the manufacturer directly online while at the RAM manufacturer's web site.

# Plugging in RAM

RAM is literally plug-and-play. It is important that your computer be unplugged from electricity and that you are well grounded, to avoid static-shocking any of the components inside the computer. Avoid touching the inside of a computer while standing on carpeting for this reason. Static electricity can cause damage to electrical components, even if you don't feel the static shock. You can purchase an anti-static wrist strap (highly recommended) for less than $10 at most computer/ electronics retail stores, and you should wear it whenever working on components inside a computer.

Be aware that each computer has a limited number of sockets available to add RAM modules. If there are three sockets and they are all filled, you will need to remove one of the RAM modules to make room for your new one. Also, some RAM modules are incompatible with each other, even though they are the right type of

RAM for your computer. For this reason, I recommend that you purchase RAM in the largest size available for your system that you can afford and remove all old RAM to avoid these problems.

When plugging the RAM into the computer, it will only go in facing a certain direction. Be careful to line up the notch on the RAM module with the notch on the socket. Each side of the RAM module should click into place when seated properly.

The detailed steps for adding RAM vary depending on the type of RAM your computer requires. RAM is sold as an OEM (original equipment manufacturer) product, or as a retail "boxed" product. While you may save money purchasing OEM RAM, it will not come with any instructions. OEM implies that the product is intended to be sold to PC manufacturers and therefore does not contain any instructions or retail packaging. It is generally sold as a memory stick in an anti-static bag. Nothing more, nothing less.

Retail boxed RAM will contain actual plastic packaging around the product along with detailed instructions on how to install the RAM. Because the installation varies slightly depending on the type of RAM your computer requires, I recommend purchasing the retail boxed RAM and following the instructions that come with it. While the retail boxed RAM will cost a few dollars more, for a novice, it's worth the slight added cost for the detailed and helpful installation documentation.

For more information on how to install RAM, please visit www.pny.com/install/desktop.asp.

Once your RAM is installed, be sure to test it and verify that all of your computer's memory is recognized by your system using Memtest86, a free tool that you can download from www.memtest86.com. If the RAM fails any test, exchange it for a new RAM module immediately.

# Upgrading Your Monitor

Many people want to buy the fastest computer with as many bells and whistles as possible, but then they get a cheap monitor.

The monitor is the single most important part of your computer. Your computer is completely worthless without it. You can purchase any new monitor, without worrying about compatibility problems. All new monitors will work with your PC; however, an older monitor may not work with a newer PC.

## What's the Viewable Area?

Monitors are measured diagonally, and the glass tube, or CRT (Cathode-Ray Tube), in a monitor is measured before it is installed in the plastic casing. A glass monitor typically has about an inch of the screen that is behind the plastic and cannot be seen. For this reason, a glass monitor that measures 17 inches will typically have a 15.9-inch *viewable area.*

Liquid crystal display (LCD) monitors do not have any lost screen area. Thus, a 15-inch LCD monitor actually displays 15 inches (imagine that!). A 15-inch LCD monitor has a viewable area that is similar to that of a 17-inch glass monitor.

## LCD or Glass?

Even though LCD monitors are all the rage, they are not recommended for people who like to play action games. Although the technology is improving, most LCD screens simply do not refresh the screen information fast enough, resulting in fast images leaving a trail. For example, if you were watching a tennis match on a typical LCD screen, the tennis ball would appear to have a tail as it streaked across the screen. The high-end LCD monitors have solved this problem, but they are cost-prohibitive for most people.

On the other hand, if you work for hours on end in front of your computer dealing mainly with text, you may find that an LCD monitor is easier on your eyes and on your electric bill. It also frees up quite a bit of space on the top of your desk.

 *Purchasing a very inexpensive LCD monitor may result in poor image quality. Just because it's an LCD monitor doesn't automatically make it better.*

There are now flat-glass monitors that have great picture quality with no distortion, and they are offered at a fraction of the cost of LCD monitors. I recommend a 19-inch flat-glass monitor for price and picture quality balance.

When shopping for a glass monitor, look for the smallest dot pitch and highest refresh rate. The smaller the dot pitch, the sharper the image. When shopping for an LCD monitor, look for a higher-contrast ratio (for example, 450:1 is much better then 300:1). Some high-end LCD monitors also require a special video card with a DVI (digital visual interface) connector. Only high-end LCD monitors require this type of connector, so unless you have a high-end LCD monitor now, chances are you want an LCD monitor that has a standard analog video connector and not a DVI. Be aware that some high-end LCD monitors have the capability to use either type of connector.

In addition, most monitors from major manufacturers come with a three-year warranty. Although you might save money buying a no-name brand monitor, consider anything less then a three-year warranty suspect.

For more information about monitors, visit http://computer.howstuffworks.com/monitor.htm.

Finally, don't let anyone tell you which monitor is better than another. Let your eyes decide. Each individual's eyes are unique. If you cannot see a difference between a $250 monitor and a $700 monitor, purchase the cheaper one!

# Upgrading Your CPU

If you're considering upgrading your computer's CPU (central processing unit) to something faster and more modern, it will probably require a new motherboard, new memory, and a new CPU fan, along with the new CPU. It may also require a new, more powerful power supply (new CPUs require 300 watts minimum), a new video card, and a new hard disk. If you fail to upgrade these last two components when upgrading your CPU, your system will be no faster than the slowest component. Hence, you might as well just replace the computer.

It rarely makes sense to upgrade a CPU. The easiest CPU upgrades are when you are upgrading within 12 months of purchasing your computer. Since the upgrade is a minor boost in speed, and the computer is still relatively fast and new, most people don't think it's worth the trouble. As time progresses, however, manufacturers will have improved other components as well, and upgrading the CPU is no longer enough.

# Upgrading Your Hard Disk

A hard disk that spins at 7,200 rotations per minute (RPM) will transfer data faster and actually run quieter than the old 5,400 RPM hard disks. Also, modern hard disks have large onboard caches available to help speed up the transfer of data. It's not uncommon to find a modern hard disk that has an 8MB cache built into it. Quite often, manufacturers will offer a hard disk with or without this 8MB cache, and the difference in price is usually less than $20. This cache allows the hard disk to operate faster, and many hard disk manufacturers offer a three-year warranty on the hard disks that have the 8MB cache option, while offering only a one-year warranty on the hard disks without the cache.

Hard disks can be tricky and confusing to install, and there are numerous limitations on hard disk size that are associated with the age of your computer. For example, there was no such thing as a consumer-based 40GB hard disk in 1998. As a result, a computer purchased in 1998 will not be able to recognize a 40GB hard disk without a lot of technical help. Consider the following limitations:

■ Early 486 computers cannot see any hard disk greater than 528MB in size.

■ Later 486 computers and Pentium I computers cannot see any hard disk greater than 2GB in size.

■ Later Pentium I computers can recognize a maximum hard disk of 8GB.

■ Many systems built before 1999 cannot see hard disks larger than 32GB.

■ Most modern computers cannot recognize a hard disk greater than 127GB in size.

So, if you have an old Pentium II computer, upgrading its hard disk to a new 120GB hard disk may not be possible. The technology that exists today to allow 120GB hard disks did not exist years ago when that computer was designed.

Also, transferring data from one hard disk to another, as well as configuring disks to work together, can be very complicated. For this reason, I recommend seeking the help of a professional if you're considering replacing or adding another hard disk to your system.

Finally, keeping an old hard disk attached to a new hard disk will slow down the new hard disk. If you want to take as much advantage of the new hard disk as your system will allow, be sure to leave the old hard disk out of your system once the new hard disk is installed. Of course, this varies depending on just how old your "old" hard disk is. A professional technician can advise you if your old hard disk is worth keeping.

# Upgrade Your Internet Connection

If you spend a lot of time on the Internet, you may find that having high-speed Internet connection allows you to accomplish much more in much less time. Many people have a second phone line ($20 a month) and pay for their Internet access ($22 a month). Consider that you could spend $45 a month to get a connection that is as much as 100 times faster, is less frustrating, and keeps your phone line free.

Some people think that they don't need a high-speed connection. They say, "I just use the Internet for simple things like e-mail and some web surfing." Of course that's all they use it for! Anything else is too frustrating and time-consuming. After they have a high-speed connection available, the way they use the Internet will change.

Once you get used to having high-speed Internet access, you'll wonder how you ever got along with dial-up access as long as you did—no more disconnects, no more busy signals, and no more waiting.

TIP *If you currently have America Online (AOL), you can get high-speed Internet access and still keep your AOL account, but cut your monthly fee from AOL in half. Call AOL and say that you won't be needing to dial in to AOL (freeing up the phone lines for other members). Then you can access AOL directly through your high-speed Internet provider. AOL will discount your monthly rate by more than 50 percent as a result. Everybody wins!*

# Replacing Your Computer

If your computer was built before the year 2000, it's probably best to think about purchasing a new computer rather than putting any money into a PC that old. Computers running slower than 800MHz should also be considered for replacement, rather than upgrading.

## Limitations of Proprietary Computers

Major manufacturers such as Dell, Hewlett-Packard, Gateway, and E-machines build many of their systems using proprietary components. This means that no one else can provide you replacement parts except that specific manufacturer. This may not be an issue while your machine is under warranty, but once your warranty expires, it becomes important. For example, a simple $30 power supply in most computers is an $80 power supply from Dell. Any other type of power supply may simply not fit or, in some cases, could cause a fire!

Many of the major manufacturers use a marketing gimmick called *shared memory*. This is when the video card is built into the motherboard, rather than being a modular (removable) circuit board that can be unplugged and replaced. Using shared memory means that the video card has no memory of its own and it must "share" your main RAM. Thus, if you have 128MB of RAM installed in your computer, but your video card is reserving 8MB for its use, only 120MB will be available to Windows. That doesn't sound like the definition of sharing that I am familiar with; that sounds more like stealing. The result is that a system with a shared memory video card will run slower than an equivalent system with a modular video card.

## Which Computer Should I Get?

If you see two computers at the store with the same specifications but a different price, I can assure you the cheaper computer either runs slower or has less of a warranty (or both). Having a computer built to meet your needs is preferred, but there are risks: some shops go out of business, leaving you with no warranty, or they may sell you inferior components.

Ask around and get opinions from friends. If they know of a local small business owner who has treated them well, get a price comparison and don't be afraid to ask questions. In many cases, knowing a decent small business owner can be like having your own trusted doctor or mechanic. There is a level of personal service that the large corporations simply cannot offer.

On the other hand, if you feel more comfortable with a major brand name computer, ask the company representatives if they sell computers that do not have proprietary components (so you can customize every aspect of the computer). See what the price difference is. If a proprietary computer is all you can afford, be sure you are aware of its limitations before making the purchase.

Finally, check out www.epinions.com to look up reviews by typical buyers like yourself. You can find information about computer manufacturers and the individual models of computers you are considering purchasing. When you do make that purchase, you are welcome to leave a review of your experience at epinions.com to let others know and help them in their future purchasing decisions. It's free and offers critiques from "real people" on everything from restaurants to vacation spots to electronic gizmos and even movies.

# Summary

In this chapter, you've learned all about the upgrade possibilities available to you. Decisions, decisions!

The next chapter presents some practical performance and tune-up tips. You'll learn how to blow out the dust and dog/cat hair from inside your PC, ensure that all of your cooling fans are operating properly, and even delete temporary files manually (Windows has a reputation for leaving numerous temporary files untouched during its automated removal process).

You're almost finished. At the rate you're going, you'll soon be ready to start teaching others!

# Part IV

## Advanced Topics

# Chapter 11

# Preventive Maintenance

Aside from everything you've already accomplished thus far throughout this book, there are additional steps you can take to ensure that your computer continues to run trouble-free. Removing dust and debris from inside the computer on a regular basis, as well as looking for early indications of problems, can help you stay one step ahead of your computer failures.

This chapter will show you what to look for and what to do to keep your computer running in tip-top shape.

# Maintain Computer Parts

Like any other physical item, over time, your computer gets dusty. You will need to remove the computer case to get rid of the dust. While you have the computer case off, you can check two other computer parts: the fans and the capacitors.

## Blow Out Dust and Debris

As your computer is running, air is moved through the system to help keep it cool. Ironically, this air also brings with it dust and pet hair, which act as an insulator, causing the components that they collect on to run hotter. In extreme cases, this additional heat can be responsible for system instability or even permanent failure.

For this reason, it's imperative that you open the computer case and blow out this dust and debris. Computer cases all open uniquely. Some have screws in the back that allow the cover to be removed. Others, such as Dell computers, require no tools and simply snap open with the press of a lever. Some require the face of the computer to be removed to reveal the screws holding the cover on. On some old Packard Bell computers, screws from the bottom of the case needed to be removed to get the side panels off. Some computers have individual panels on the left and the right; others, such as some Dell computers, open on a hinge while others may open by removing the entire outer shell.

Be sure to have everything unplugged before attempting to remove any covers or side panels, and never force anything. Everything should fit snuggly, but not to a point that it requires excessive force. If you cannot determine how to open your computer case, this process may be best left to a professional.

Once you have the inside of the computer exposed, use a can of compressed air (which can be purchased from any electronics or computer store) to blow out the dust and debris. You may want to take the PC outside prior to doing this to keep your house clean. Be sure to remove dust from the fans and power supply, where it tends to collect the most. Do not spray the air into your floppy drive or CD-ROM drives, because the force with which it comes out could damage them. Spray the inside of the PC only, and continue to spray until you no longer see clouds of dust coming out.

## Ensure All Fans Are Operating Properly

While you have the computer cover removed, temporarily hook up the PC and turn it on. With the power on, visually inspect all of the cooling fans. They should spin freely without stuttering or stalling. If any of the fans inside your computer fail to spin or are not spinning with consistency, plan on getting those fans replaced as soon as possible. When fans are not spinning freely as they should, your computer will run hotter than normal. If a fan has completely failed, chances are your computer will fail, too. Proper cooling is essential. Today's CPUs run at temperatures of 120 to 190 degrees Fahrenheit, and that is when they *are* being properly cooled!

If you hear a grinding noise and want to determine which fan is causing the disturbance, use any plastic tool to force the fan to stop while it is running. Do not do this excessively. Stop the fan only long enough to determine if the noise stops, which should take less than two seconds. Using plastic will ensure that you will not receive an electric shock. Be careful not to touch any of the electronics in the computer while performing this diagnostic.

Be aware that some video cards also have fans, and those fans are not easily viewed. Accelerated Graphics Port (AGP) video cards mount upside-down. You may need to get down on your knees to position yourself, and use a flashlight to inspect a video card fan. The AGP video card, if you have one, is always the first card, closest to the top of the computer.

If you discover that the fan in your power supply is not spinning or is making noise, it is recommended that you replace the entire power supply. Working inside a power supply can be dangerous. Even with the power off, there are components that store electricity within a power supply (called *capacitors*) that can electrocute you. A power supply is fairly inexpensive and usually pretty straightforward to replace. Do not attempt to replace the fan inside a power supply, or otherwise open a power supply for any reason. There are no user-serviceable parts inside a power supply. Simply unplug the computer, unplug all of the internal power connectors that come from the power supply, remove the screws that hold the power supply in place from the back of your PC, and replace it with one of a similar design and capacity.

## Verify That the Capacitors on the Motherboard Are Not Leaking

Many computers sold from 2000 to 2002 were manufactured with defective capacitors. Thus far, only two manufacturers have admitted it (Abit and IBM); others prefer to act as if they have no idea about this problem.

A leaking capacitor may not cause any system problems at first, but over time, as more and more electrolyte leaks out, the computer may behave erratically, lock up, be completely unusable, or even, in the most catastrophic cases, start to smoke and catch fire.

A capacitor looks similar to a small battery. When it leaks, it looks similar to a leaking battery.

While you have your computer case off, use a flashlight to inspect the capacitors. Look for any bulging or leakage from the top and bottom of all capacitors, as shown in Figure 11-1. Do not come in contact with any of the leakage. If you

**FIGURE 11-1**    Leaking capacitors

should accidentally get the leaking electrolyte on your skin, immediately wash the affected area thoroughly with soap and water. Although the electrolyte is probably harmless, it's always better to be safe than sorry. Don't worry—the electrolyte won't spray out at you. The only way you will get electrolyte on your skin is if you touch it or brush against the leaking capacitor.

If you find bulging or leaking capacitors, your computer's main board, or *motherboard*, will need to be replaced. If your system is under warranty, this replacement will be done at no charge. It's important that you inspect your computer early and often for this problem so that you're not stuck with the repair bill.

NOTE
*The motherboard is the largest circuit board in your PC. All the other circuit boards plug into the motherboard (main board), as do the RAM and CPU.*

If you would like to learn more about this phenomenon, visit my web site at www.careyholzman.com for pictures and in-depth articles about how and why this happens, along with the latest news on class-action lawsuits being brought against specific manufacturers.

# Download the Latest Drivers

A *driver* is a piece of software that instructs Windows how to communicate with a specific piece of hardware. Your printer has a driver, as does your video card, sound card, and even some motherboards. From time to time, the manufacturers of the hardware optimize their drivers and improve their efficiency and reliability. However, you won't know if there are any updated drivers for your hardware unless you check for yourself.

A prime example of a company that updates its drivers quite often is NVIDIA, the video card manufacturer. If you own one of the very popular GeForce video cards, chances are you are running an old, outdated driver.

Many people find that their computers run smoother, crash less often and, in many cases, operate faster after updating a major driver, such as the video card. The original driver may have had bugs or other issues associated with it that were repaired in later versions of the driver. Updated drivers typically fix problems and work more efficiently and cooperatively within Windows than older versions.

If your system is running just fine and you have no complaints, then don't "fix" it. On the other hand, if your system is unstable or slow (or both), or you would just like it to run a little faster, consider updating your drivers.

## Checking Your Current Drivers

To help you determine what brand and model of hardware you have, as well as what version driver you are running, we'll step through the process, using your video card as a primary example.

1. Windows 98/Me users, click **Start**, click **Settings**, and click **Control Panel**. Windows XP users, click **Start** and click **Control Panel**.

2. Double-click the **System** icon.

3. Windows 98/Me users, click the **Device Manager** tab. Windows XP users, click the **Hardware** tab, and then click the **Device Manager** button located in the center of the window.

4. Click the + symbol next to **Display adapters**. The name and type of your video card will appear, as shown in Figure 11-2. In this example, the video card is manufactured by a company called STB, and the model of the card is called a Velocity 128.

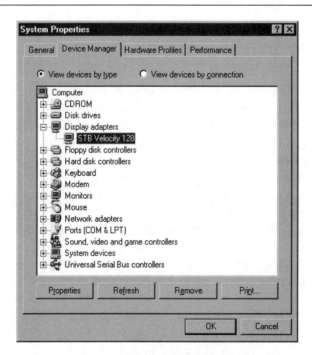

**FIGURE 11-2**   Determining your video card in Windows 98/Me

**5.** Double-click the name of the video card that appears. The **Properties** dialog box will open.

**6.** Click the **Driver** tab, and then click the **Driver File Details...** button if you are running Windows 98/Me, or click the **Driver Details...** button if you are running Windows XP. This window will display the driver files and their version number, as shown in Figure 11-3. In this example, we are running version 4.10.01.7194.

# Checking for New Drivers

After you've gotten the details about the driver installed on your computer, visit the manufacturer's web site to see the latest version of the driver available. The following are some common video card manufacturers' sites:

- NVIDIA, www.nvidia.com

- ATI, www.ati.com

- S3 Graphics, www.s3graphics.com

- SiS, www.sis.com

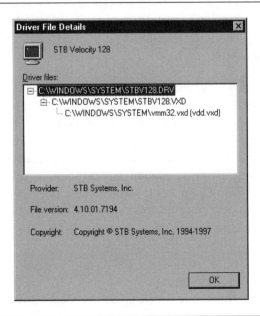

FIGURE 11-3    Determining the version of a driver in Windows 98/Me

If your card manufacturer is not listed here, try using the Google search engine to look for the make and model of your card. In this example, we'll visit **www.google.com**, and type **STB Velocity 128 Driver Download** in the search box, and then click **Search**. The search will reveal either the location of the company, or other web sites that may contain the driver you're looking for, should the company no longer be in business.

In some cases, you may not be able to find your video card manufacturer's web site. For example, the manufacturer of the video card shown in Figures 11-2 and 11-3, STB, used to be located at www.stb.com; however, the company has long since gone out of business, and no newer drivers are available. Also, if you have a Voodoo card or Diamond MultiMedia card, you won't have much luck reaching their web site, because those are other companies that have gone out of business.

If the version number of the available driver is higher than the version you currently have, it would be wise to update the driver. Follow the manufacturer's specific instructions to update your drivers. If you are having a difficult time understanding the version numbers, you could always download and install the latest driver available from the manufacturer just to make sure you have the newest driver installed on your computer.

Aside from video cards, other companies such as Iomega (who manufactures the Zip drive) also update their drivers quite frequently.

If your motherboard has a VIA chipset, visit www.viaarena.com and download and install the latest VIA 4in1 drivers. If you are uncertain if your computer has a VIA chipset, the next time you have the cover off and are blowing out the dust, look for any chips on the motherboard that say *VIA* on them. If you spot one, you have a VIA-based motherboard.

> NOTE
>
> *If this seems too complicated, you can try visiting www.drivershq.com and run their Driver Detective. It automates the process, removing all the guess work. It will report when updates are available; however, it will cost you $29.95 a year to actually get the updates from them. You can also download a utility called DriverMagic, available from www .rubymicro.com/drivermagic.html, but, once again, you must pay for this service. Finally, as a last resort, you can visit www.driverguide.com, which is completely free and has a vast resource of drivers from numerous manufacturers.*

If you have an Intel CPU, chances are you do not have a VIA-based main board. If you have an AMD CPU, chances are you do have a VIA-based main board, although you should check to verify before installing the VIA 4in1 driver.

*Be very careful when updating drivers. Selecting and installing the wrong driver can cause severe system problems. If you install the wrong driver by mistake and you are using Windows Me or XP, use the System Restore feature to return your computer back in time, as explained in Chapter 12. If this process makes you nervous, don't update your drivers.*

# Removing Temp Files Manually

In the first chapter of this book, you learned how to instruct Windows to automatically delete the temp files. Now that you are more familiar with your PC, your operating system, and how to navigate it, you're ready to learn how to manually remove the temp files Windows leaves behind, even after you've instructed it to remove them.

Unfortunately, Windows deletes only the temp files it's familiar with and will leave all other temp files alone. Because other programs within Windows create temp files, you need to remove those files manually. Over time, those files can take up quite a bit of hard disk space. Since the program that used these temp files has long since abandoned them, it's always safe to delete them.

## Deleting Temp Files in Windows XP Systems

The following steps show how to delete temp files manually on a Windows XP computer. If, during this process, you receive an error message that the file cannot be deleted or access is denied, that simply means that one (or more) of the temp files you are trying to erase is currently in use by Windows. Take note of the name of the file, close the error message box, and then look through the list of files to find the one that caused the error. All of the files should remain highlighted and typically the file you're looking for will be at or near the top of the list. While holding down the CTRL button on your keyboard, click that file to deselect it (while leaving the others highlighted). You may need to repeat this process several times.

Before we begin, we need to determine what name you are logged into the computer as. It may be your name, or maybe a generic name depending on who initially set up your computer when you first got it. To determine what your user name is, click **Start**, click **Run** and type **taskmgr** and click **OK**. Click the very last tab labeled Users; the name listed under Users is the name you are logged in as.

Once you've determined your user name, close the Task Manager window by clicking on the X in the upper-right corner of the window.

NOTE

*If the name you are logged in to Windows XP with is not your name, don't worry. The name can be anything. The only reason we need to know it now is to locate where your temp files are stored. For a shortcut to this information, click the Internet Options icon in the Control Panel and click the Settings button. In the middle of the window that appears you'll see Current Location: C:\Documents and Settings\. Make a note of this info, as this is where you will need to go to manually remove temp files.*

1. Double-click the **My Computer** icon, and then double-click the **C:** drive.

2. You may receive a warning message that says, "These files are hidden. This folder contains files that keep your system working properly. You should not modify its contents." Figure 11-4 shows the Local Disk (C:) window with this message. As long as you follow the instructions in this book, there will be no danger. Click **Show the contents of this folder**.

3. Double-click the **Documents and Settings** folder.

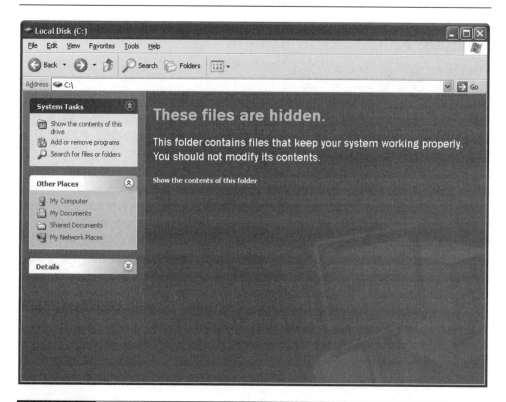

**FIGURE 11-4** Windows XP warning message when attempting to access files on the hard disk

4. Locate the folder with your logon name and double-click it (do not select the **Default User** or **All Users** folder).

5. In the menu bar at the top of the window, click **Tools**, and then click **Folder Options**.

6. Click the **View** tab. Make sure **Show hidden files and folders** is selected, as shown in Figure 11-5, and then click **OK**.

7. Double-click the **Local Settings** folder, and then double-click the **Temp** folder.

8. In the menu bar at the top of the window, click **View**, click **Arrange Icons by**, and click **Type**.

9. Scroll through the list to find the first file that ends with **.tmp** and click it. Continue scrolling through the list and, while holding down the SHIFT key, click the last file that ends in **.tmp**. This will select all of the .tmp files.

10. Press the DELETE key on your keyboard.

11. When finished, close any open windows.

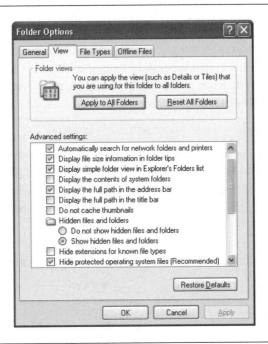

**FIGURE 11-5**    Windows XP View settings

## Deleting Temp Files in Windows Me Systems

The following steps show how to delete temp files manually on a Windows Me computer. If an error occurs during this process, it simply means that one or more of the temp files you are trying to remove is currently in use by Windows. Take note of the name of the file, close the error message box, and then look through the list of files to find the one that caused the error. All of the files should remain highlighted, and, typically, the file you're looking for will be at or near the top of the list. While holding down the CTRL key on your keyboard, click that file to deselect it (while leaving the others highlighted). If you make a mistake, you can start over by holding down the CTRL key and pressing the A key on your keyboard. This is a keyboard shortcut that will highlight (select) all of the files.

Once the file is deselected, try again to delete the remaining files. If another error message occurs, take note of that file and deselect it as well. Repeat this process as necessary. There are typically no more than eight files currently in use, so don't get frustrated if you get the error message a couple of times. And remember that the files will most likely be easy to find, because they should be at the top of the list.

1.  Double-click the **My Computer** icon, and then double-click on the **C:** drive.

2.  Click **View**, located in the menu bar at the top of the window, and click **List.**

3.  Click **View** (again), click **Arrange Icons**, and click **By Name**.

4.  The contents of the C: drive should be displayed alphabetically (the yellow folders are alphabetized separately from the files). If the window opens without any content, as shown in Figure 11-6, click **View the entire contents of this drive**.

5.  Double-click the yellow folder named **Windows**.

6.  You may receive a warning message that says, "This folder contains files that keep your computer working properly. Please be careful if you modify the contents of this folder." As long as you follow the instructions in this book, there will be no danger. Click **View the entire contents of this folder**.

7.  Click **View**, and then click **List**.

8.  Click **View**, click **Arrange Icons**, and click **By Name**.

9.  Double-click the yellow folder named **TEMP**.

10. Click **View**, and then click **List**.

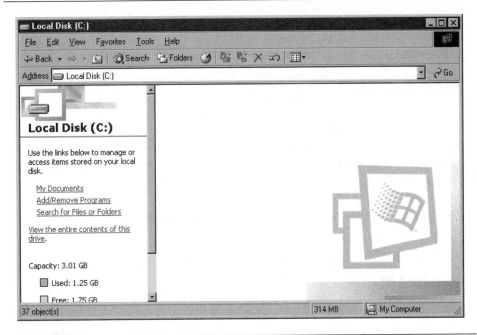

**FIGURE 11-6**    Windows Me hiding the contents of the C: drive

11. Click **Tools**, and then click **Folder Options…**.

12. Click the **View** tab. Make sure **Show hidden files and folders** is selected. Also ensure that the option (located right below it) **Hide file extensions for known file types** is unchecked. Then click **OK**.

13. Click **Edit**, and then click **Select All** (you should see the entire contents of this folder highlighted).

14. Press the DELETE key on your keyboard. Click **Yes** when asked if you are sure.

15. Close the window.

# Deleting Temp Files in Windows 98 Systems

The following steps show how to delete temp files manually on a Windows 98 computer. If an error occurs during this process, it simply means that one (or more) of the temp files you are trying to remove is currently in use by Windows. Take note of the name of the file, close the error message box, and then look through the list of files to find the one that caused the error. All of the files should remain highlighted, and, typically, the file you're looking for will be at or near the top of the list. While holding down the CTRL key on your keyboard, click that file, and it should be deselected (while leaving the others highlighted). If you make a mistake, you can start over by holding down the CTRL key and pressing the A key on your keyboard. This is a keyboard shortcut that will highlight (select) all of the files.

Once the file is deselected, try again to delete the remaining files. If another error message occurs, take note of that file and deselect it as well. Repeat this process as necessary. There should not be more then five files currently in use, so don't get frustrated if you get the error message a couple of times. And remember that the files will most likely be easy to find, because they should be at the top of the list.

1.  Double-click the **My Computer** icon, and then double-click on the **C:** drive.

2.  Click **View**, located in the menu bar at the top of the window, and then click **List.**

3.  Click **View** (again), click **Arrange Icons**, and click **By Name**.

4.  The contents of the C: drive should be displayed alphabetically (the yellow folders are alphabetized separately from the files). Double-click the yellow folder named **Windows**.

5.  You may receive a warning message that says, "Modifying the contents of this folder may cause your programs to stop working correctly." Of course, if you follow the directions in this book, modifying the contents as instructed may cause your programs to *start* working correctly. So, click **Show Files**.

6.  Click **View**, and then click **List.**

7.  Click **View**, and then click **Folder Options....**

8.  Click the **View** tab. Make sure **Show all files** is selected. Also ensure that the option (located right below it) **Hide file extensions for known file types** is unchecked, as shown in Figure 11-7. Then click **OK**.

9.  Double-click the yellow folder named **Temp**. (Depending on your computer configuration, you may have to select **Show Files** again, as explained in step 5.)

10. Click **View**, and then click **List.**

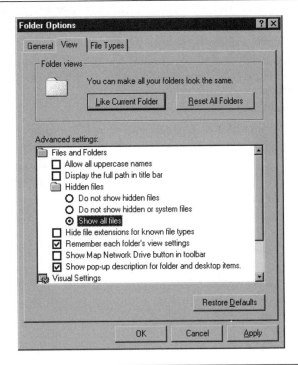

**FIGURE 11-7**   Windows 98 View options

**11.** Click **View** (again), click **Arrange Icons**, and click **By Name**.

**12.** Click **Edit**, and then click **Select All** (you should see the entire contents of this folder highlighted).

**13.** Press the DELETE key on your keyboard. Click **Yes** when asked if you are sure.

**14.** Close the window.

# Summary

In this chapter, you've learned how to remove the dust and debris from inside your computer to help keep it running cooler, as well as what to check for early detection of failing components. You also learned how and why to update device drivers, and how to manually locate and remove those pesky temp files Windows leaves behind. Being proactive with your PC maintenance will ensure your PC remains as reliable and responsive as possible.

In the next and final chapter, you'll learn what to do when things go wrong before calling a technician and spending any money. Using built-in Windows features to take your computer back in time to when it was working properly can resolve most software issues. The next chapter will introduce you to some problem resolution options you may not know exist.

Hang in there! You're almost finished, and your PC couldn't be happier or healthier, thanks to you!

# Chapter 12

## What to Do When Things Go Wrong

When good computers go bad, it can be a frustrating experience trying to set things right. To help with this problem, Windows Me includes a great utility called System Restore. With System Restore, the computer automatically protects its own critical files and backs up the Windows Registry at regular intervals, all by itself. Microsoft improved System Restore with the release of Windows XP, allowing an even greater chance of returning your computer to a working and reliable state.

Another helpful tool for finding out what is wrong with your computer is Safe Mode, which starts up your computer with only the necessary Windows components loaded. Safe Mode is available to Windows 98, Windows Me, and Windows XP users.

In this chapter, you'll learn how to use System Restore and Safe Mode to rescue your computer when things go wrong. You'll also learn what software to *never* install on your system.

# System Restore

Wouldn't it be nice if you could send your crashed computer back in time to when it was working correctly? Well, Windows Me and Windows XP users can do this, thanks to a Microsoft feature called System Restore, included with those operating systems.

## What Does System Restore Do?

Using System Restore, you can restore your computer to the *last-known good Windows configuration*; in other words, to the same state it was in the last time it was working correctly. If your computer suddenly stops working properly, simply start System Restore.

When you start System Restore and choose to repair your computer, a calendar appears, showing you all of the *restore points* that have been made. Choose the date closest to the time that you know the computer was operating properly, and the computer configuration will be resurrected to the same condition it was in on that day.

If your system suddenly won't start Windows properly, try booting into Safe Mode (following the steps in the "Safe Mode" section later in this chapter), and then use System Restore while in Safe Mode. In many cases, if you are not having a hardware problem, your system will work just as it did on the restore date you selected.

You should know that the System Restore utility monitors only critical Windows files and specific Windows configuration files, such as the Registry. It will not recover lost data, nor will it erase any data that was created after the restore point date you select. Simply put, it changes only the condition of Windows. If you installed a program yesterday, and you restore to the day before yesterday, the data will remain, but Windows will be returned to a state prior to that software being installed. Then you can install that software once again, but you might not want to if it was the cause of your problems.

> TIP
>
> *You can also create your own restore points manually (in addition to the ones that Windows creates for you automatically). For example, you might want to do this prior to installing any new software on your computer. To make a restore point, click **Start**, then **Programs,** then **Accessories**, then **System Tools**, then **System Restore**. In the System Restore window, select **Create a restore point** and follow the simple onscreen directions.*

## Using System Restore (for Windows Me/XP Users)

To run System Restore on a Windows Me or Windows XP computer, follow these steps:

1. Click **Start**, click **Programs**, click **Accessories**, and click **System Tools**.

2. Click **System Restore**.

3. In the window that appears, select **Restore my computer to an earlier time**, as shown in Figure 12-1, and then click **Next**.

4. The next window displays a calendar with dates on which restore points have been made in bold print, as shown in Figure 12-2. If you click once on a bold date, a brief description of that restore point will be displayed. Choose the nearest date that you know your computer was working properly and click **Next**.

5. The next window that appears warns you to close any open programs and to verify that you want to execute this procedure. Windows Me users will need to click **OK** to close the warning dialog box before continuing. If you are certain you want to restore your computer to the date you selected, click **Next**.

6. The computer will restore the Windows configuration back to the date you selected, and then automatically restart Windows. A message will be displayed immediately when Windows restarts, confirming the restore operation was successful. (If the restore operation failed for any reason, try booting the computer in Safe Mode and repeat this process, only try an earlier restore point.) Click **OK** to allow Windows to complete its startup routine.

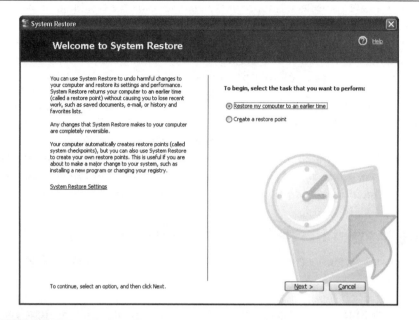

**FIGURE 12-1**   Starting System Restore in Windows Me/XP

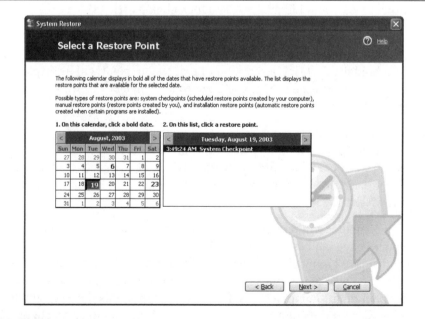

**FIGURE 12-2**   Choosing a restore point from the System Restore calendar

# Safe Mode

Windows 98, Windows Me, and Windows XP have the ability to start up in a very basic mode called Safe Mode, in which only the necessary Windows components are loaded. Starting your computer in this mode can help you to diagnose if a problem is software- or hardware-related. Safe Mode also allows many Windows 98 and Windows Me users to use the Scandisk and Defragment utilities on their hard disk without interruption (see Chapter 1 for information about using these utilities).

When your computer is in Safe Mode, the text "Safe Mode" will appear in all four corners of the screen. Also, your screen will look different, because only 16 colors will be displayed, instead of the larger display of colors you are accustomed to seeing.

The following sections describe how to configure your computer to start in Safe Mode using the MSCONFIG, or System Configuration, utility (introduced in Chapter 8), if you can start your computer into Windows normally. If this is not possible, or if you prefer, you can also start the computer in Safe Mode by repeatedly pressing the F8 key on your keyboard when you first turn on your computer, but before the Windows logo appears. Many people have a difficult time getting the timing just right for this to work properly, however. So, if you can get Windows started, try the techniques described here.

> NOTE    *You cannot install any software while in Safe Mode. Safe Mode is intended for diagnostic and repair purposes only.*

## Starting Windows 98/Me Systems in Safe Mode

If you can start the computer normally into Windows 98 or Windows Me, follow these steps to configure the computer to restart in Safe Mode:

1.  Close all windows.

2.  Click **Start**, click **Run**, and type **msconfig**, as shown in Figure 12-3. Then click **OK**.

3.  The System Configuration Utility window appears, as shown in Figure 12-4. Click the **Advanced** button.

4.  When the Advanced Troubleshooting Settings dialog box appears, place a check next to **Enable Startup Menu**, as shown in Figure 12-5. Then click **OK**.

5.  Click **OK** once more.

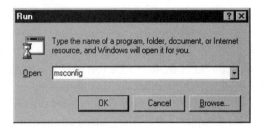

FIGURE 12-3     Running the MSCONFIG utility in Windows Me

**6.** You will be prompted to restart the computer. Click **Yes**.

**7.** When the computer restarts, a menu will appear. Select **Safe Mode** using the arrow keys on your keyboard, and then press ENTER. If you do not make a selection within 30 seconds, Windows will boot normally. When instructing the computer to start in Safe Mode, be patient—the startup process may take several minutes.

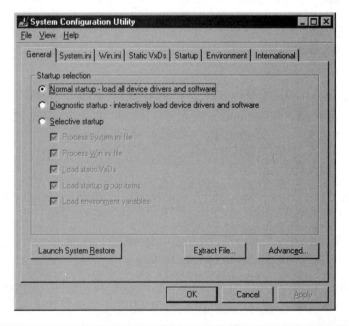

FIGURE 12-4     The System Configuration Utility window in Windows Me

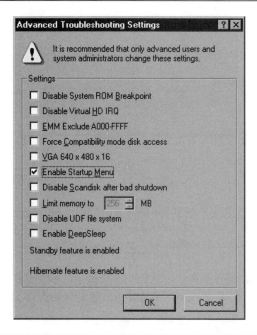

FIGURE 12-5    Enabling the Windows Me Startup menu to access Safe Mode

When you are finished with Safe Mode, repeat these steps, but in step 4, uncheck **Enable Startup Menu**, and then restart the computer when prompted.

## Starting Windows XP Systems in Safe Mode

If you can start the computer normally in Windows XP, using the MSCONFIG (System Configuration) utility is the easiest and the recommended way to restart the computer in Safe Mode. Follow these steps to run Windows XP in Safe Mode:

**1.** Close all windows.

**2.** Click **Start,** click **Run,** and type **msconfig,** as shown in Figure 12-6. Then click **OK**.

**3.** The System Configuration Utility window appears. Select the tab labeled **BOOT.INI.**

**4.** Place a check next to the **/SAFEBOOT** option, as shown in Figure 12-7, and then click **OK**.

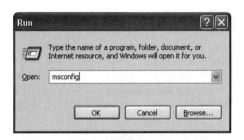

FIGURE 12-6 Running the MSCONFIG utility in Windows XP

**5.** You will be prompted to restart the computer, as shown in Figure 12-8. Click **Restart**. The computer will now restart in Safe Mode. Be patient; this may take several minutes.

When you are finished using Safe Mode, repeat these steps, but in step 4, uncheck **/SAFEBOOT**. Then close all programs and restart the computer when prompted.

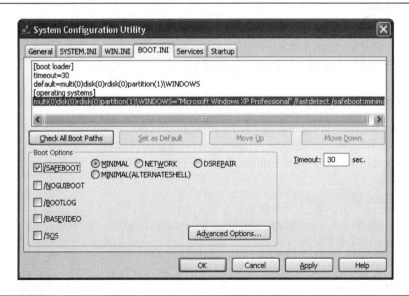

FIGURE 12-7    Choosing the /SAFEBOOT option to boot in Safe Mode in Windows XP

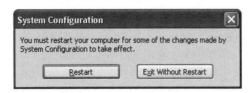

**FIGURE 12-8**   Choosing to restart the computer after selecting a Safe Mode boot

# Software to Avoid

The marketing companies would have you believe their software will fix your computer, make it run faster and more reliably, and/or make your Internet connection faster. Don't believe them.

For example, "uninstall" or "Registry cleaner" software is often touted as a remedy for correcting software problems and cleaning up your computer. However, in my experience, uninstall software is a waste of time. Registry cleaners typically cause more problems than they solve. The best any of this software can do is cover up the problem with a software band-aid. This is not only an unreliable way to fix things, but in many cases, the original problem continues to get worse and you may also have some new problems.

Stay away from purchasing software that emphasizes how much you need it. That is your first clue that you probably *don't* need it. Marketing companies tend to play with words to manipulate the perspective of value. For example, you often see the promotion "Buy one, get one free!" If you could literally get one free, then it should cost you nothing. So, they should just give you the free one. But you cannot have the free one until you purchase one first. What they really mean is, "Buy one, get one at no additional cost." This kind of deception is allowed, and most people are aware of the true meaning of "free" in these advertisements. However, promoters of many of the products advertised in email, pop-ups, and web pages on the Internet are not abiding by federal truth-in-advertising laws.

CAUTION   *Don't purchase anything you learned about from an unsolicited email! This only proves to the spammers that spamming creates more sales. This encourages them to spam even more in an effort to increase sales.*

When considering a software purchase, do some research using Google or www.epinions.com to find out if it's really worth buying. See if a demonstration version (demo) is available. By downloading and using a demo, you can discover in advance if the product is worth your hard-earned money.

# Summary

Congratulations! You've made it to the end of this book! Your PC is much healthier today than it was just a short time ago, and you've learned quite a bit through the process.

If you're feeling more confident about your computer abilities and would like to learn even more advanced tips, tweaks, and information, be sure to visit my web site at www.careyholzman.com.

If any section of this book has left you confused or you have a question that was not answered in this book, please email me directly. I would also like to hear what you thought about this book, including any critiques, suggestions, corrections, recommendations, or praise. I personally answer each email I receive and would love nothing more than to hear from you. You can reach me at Carey@CareyHolzman .com (remember that email addresses are *never* case-sensitive).

If you are eager to learn more, I highly recommend picking up a subscription to one of the two largest PC publications, *PC Magazine* or *PC World*. For less than $20 a year, you'll receive the latest PC-related news, reviews, tips, tweaks, and editorials. While some of the stories may not hold your interest, and others may be too technical, there will always be something in each issue you'll find beneficial. You can also read many of these magazines online for free. *PC Magazine's* web site can be found at www.pcmag.com and *PC World's* web site can be found at www.pcworld.com.

Thank you for purchasing this book! I hope it not only saved you a lot of money from purchasing unnecessary software, but also increased your confidence with your computer by better understanding how computers work and how to improve your computer's performance.

Since you can now appreciate nerd humor, I'll leave you with this final story:

A computer technician happens across a frog in the road. The frog pipes up, "Help me! A wicked witch has turned me into a frog. But, if you'll kiss me, I'll turn back into a beautiful princess."

The technician shrugs his shoulders, picks up the frog, and puts it in his pocket.

A few minutes later, the frog says, "Okay, if you kiss me, I'll stay with you for a month!"

The technician nods and puts the frog back in his pocket.

A few minutes later, the frog says, "Turn me back into a princess and I'll stay with you for a year and give you anything you want!"

The technician smiles and walks on.

Finally, the frog says, "What's wrong with you? I've promised to stay with you for a year and give you anything you want, and you still won't even kiss me?"

"I'm a computer technician," he replies. "I don't have time for a girlfriend. But I think having a talking frog is pretty neat!"

# Part V

# Appendixes

# Appendix A

## Free Technical Support

If you ever find yourself needing help with your computer, or if you have any computer-related questions, realize that the Internet is your best friend and resource. You can get assistance through technical support web sites, PC user groups, and Internet newsgroups.

# Technical Support Web Sites

There are several web sites dedicated to helping others. Although there are some web sites that charge for technical support, my advice is to try the free services first. The following are some web sites that offer free, courteous, friendly, and accurate technical support, with no strings attached.

- www.Protonic.com
- www.SupportFreaks.com
- www.5starsupport.com
- www.helponthe.net
- www.pctechbytes.com
- http://aumha.org
- www.CareyHolzman.com

For help with Microsoft products, visit http://support.microsoft.com and use the Microsoft Knowledge Base, where many common questions and problems are already addressed.

# PC User Groups

A *PC user group* is a group of people who attend a meeting, usually once a month, to discuss computers, have their questions answered, and learn more about PCs. There are many local PC user groups across the country.

Most user groups are free; some will ask for donations, subscriptions, or a very modest annual fee. I am not aware of any PC user group that would turn away anyone, regardless of membership dues. Membership is based on an honor system in most cases.

Most PC user groups are attended primarily by retirees looking to help one another and share their knowledge. Regardless of your age or experience, PC user groups welcome everyone. The larger organizations will even have professional presenters from companies such as Microsoft, promoting their latest software, demonstrating how it works, and offering it at a discounted price to members of the user group (often before the software is available for sale at the store). To find a PC user group in your area, visit http://www.winnetmag.com/usergroups.

# Newsgroups

Another way to find an answer to a technical problem is to use the public newsgroups. The public newsgroups are a part of the Internet where people post messages to the world at large. The posting works similar to email, except anyone can read and respond to your message. You must manually look through the newsgroup to see if anyone responded to your message; it will not arrive in your email. However, this can be one of the most satisfying and fastest ways to get a technical question answered.

Microsoft hosts its own newsgroups. To learn how to use these newsgroups, follow the directions offered at http://support.microsoft.com/newsgroups/default.aspx.

Newsgroups are not just about computers, either. There are newsgroups dedicated to discussing everything from needlepoint, to the latest episode of your favorite television show, to car repair, diseases, and genealogy. If you can imagine it, there is a group of people on the newsgroups discussing it in detail and at length.

To learn more about how newsgroups work and how to use them, visit http://computer.howstuffworks.com/newsgroup.htm.

# Appendix B

## Networking

W hat is a network? When two or more computers are connected together, this is called a *network*. When you connect to the Internet, you are becoming part of a very large network. Computers that are connected within the same building are in a LAN, or local area network. Computers that connect over a large distance are connected to a WAN, or wide area network. Numerous computers (for example, in a typical office building) are typically connected together, forming a LAN, *and* have Internet access, so they are connected to a WAN at the same time.

If you have two or more computers, you can share your Internet connection between them using a *consumer-based router*. With a consumer-based router, all computers can access your Internet connection independently and simultaneously. You can also share data files and printers between the computers. Regardless of the operating system, all PCs can be networked together.

All Windows-based computers connect very easily. Yes, if you have Windows 95 on one PC, Windows XP on another, and Windows Me on another, they will all communicate with each other (if configured properly). Although you typically cannot share programs or scanners or other hardware devices, you can transfer the data that comes from those devices from one machine to another.

Many people have opted to replace home intercom systems with Instant Messaging programs like AOL Instant Messenger (www.aim.com), MSN Messenger (http://messenger.msn.com), Yahoo Messenger (http://messenger.yahoo.com), or ICQ (www.icq.com). Sending typed messages, using a PC microphone and speakers to speak, or even using a web cam to teleconference is becoming an easy, convenient, and free way to communicate from one room in the house to another, or even across the world.

NOTE *There are very few scanners that will work over a network. They are specialty devices and cost quite a bit more than ordinary scanners for this added feature.*

Networking PCs sounds complicated, but it's actually quite simple when you follow the appropriate directions. There are numerous web sites that provide step-by-step instructions on how to set up networking, as well as troubleshooting guides for when things don't go as they should. If you're interested in learning more about how to network your home or small office, visit any of the following web sites for more information:

- www.homenethelp.com
- www.practicallynetworked.com/howto
- www.wown.com
- www.CareyHolzman.com/netfixes.htm

What's the difference between resources and memory? We briefly touch on this topic in Chapter 8. This appendix addresses the issue of system resources because it's important to understand the inherent limitations of Windows 95/98/Me to have a better overall computing experience.

If you're a person who has numerous applications open at the same time (called *multitasking*), you've probably experienced extreme system performance degradation and blue screen error messages from time to time that require you to restart your computer. We call people who frequently multitask *power users*, because they make the computer work so hard. Although adding memory to a system will help keep it responsive while multitasking, it won't help increase system resources and prevent crashes.

Windows 95/98/Me will allow only a certain number of programs to run simultaneously. This number varies, depending on how much each program taxes the operating system.

> **TIP**    *Windows 95/98/Me users can use a tool that comes with Windows called the Resource Meter. When activated, this tool acts like a fuel gauge for resources. It constantly monitors and reports your resource usage in a small graphic display next to your clock in the system tray. Of course, running it consumes resources (ironic, isn't it?), but not many. You can learn more about this tool and how to activate it at www.computerbits.com/archive/2000/0800/resourcemeter.html.*

System resources are one of the most misunderstood aspects of PCs. Even most PC technicians do not understand that system resources cannot be adjusted in Windows 95/98/Me. Some individuals may be "clever" enough to "hack" Windows and thumb their noses at such limitations, but these hacks always come at a price of reliability and performance. Windows internal modifications made by such individuals not only violate Microsoft's license agreement, but ultimately are not helping anyone when things start to go wrong.

Unfortunately, the system resource limitations with Windows 95/98/Me have no easy, reliable workaround or fix. Spending money on more memory or a larger hard disk will only affect the speed of the computer. If your computer is crashing because it is running out of resources, adding memory will only allow it to crash faster. The only way to fix this is to either not run so many programs at the same time or to upgrade your operating system to Windows 2000 or XP.

If you are currently using Windows 95/98/Me, it would behoove you to understand more about system resources and how the operating system is affected by them.

The following web sites have some great, easy-to-understand information on this topic:

- www.windows-help.net/techfiles/win-resources.html
- http://aumha.org/win4/a/resource.htm
- www.annoyances.org/exec/show/article07-104
- http://home.cfl.rr.com/bjp/Resources.htm

# Appendix D

## Windows 98/Me Help!

This appendix contains a brief compilation of the most common Windows 98/ Me problems and their possible solutions.

**How can I turn off that annoying error reporting with Internet Explorer 6 in Windows 98/Me?**

See this Microsoft Knowledge Base article at http://support.microsoft.com/ ?kbid=276550.

**I keep getting a buffer error while recording a CD with my CD-Recorder in Windows 98/Me.**

Download and install Cacheman from www.outertech.com. It has an optimized cache setting for CD burning.

**When I right-click with the mouse, the system requests a disk be inserted into drive A (a floppy disk drive).**

Do you have a program called StuffIt installed? If so, you can find the fix at www.aladdinsys.com/support/techsupport/win/dswin/dswin3.html.

**Every time I right-click the mouse on any file or folder, it always activates my floppy drive.**

See this Microsoft Knowledge Base article at http://support.microsoft.com/ ?kbid=216752.

**Every time the computer is turned on, the Scandisk program runs.**

See this Microsoft Knowledge Base article at http://support.microsoft.com/ ?kbid=273017.

**How can I turn off the annoying floating toolbar in Internet Explorer 6?**

In the Control Panel, double-click **Internet Options**, and click the **Advanced** tab. Scroll down the list to the **Multimedia** heading, and uncheck the box that says **Enable Image Toolbar**.

**Anytime I awaken my computer when the screensaver is running, there will be an empty box in the Taskbar.**

This box goes away when you click it, but in most cases, you can clear this up by updating your video drivers. You can also try reducing the Hardware Acceleration setting for your display adapter, as follows:

1. Right-click **My Computer**, click **Properties**, and then click the **Performance** tab.

2. Click the **Graphics** button, and then move the **Hardware Acceleration** slider two notches to the left.

3. Click **OK**, click **Close**, and then click **Yes** to restart your computer.

**My image preview has just decided to stop previewing images!**

To repair image view, click **Start**, click **Run**, type **regsvr32 thumbvw.dll**, and click **OK**. Image preview should now work correctly.

**Why does my computer take forever to update hardware information?**

This problem is caused by an incompatibility with Symantec's Norton System Doctor and Windows Me. Norton System Doctor creates several thousand zero-byte files in your C:\Windows\Inf directory. You must delete these zero-byte files. More information on this problem and how to prevent it from occurring in the future can be found at http://support.microsoft.com/?kbid=281967.

**How can I change Internet Explorer's small buttons back to the larger buttons?**

In **Internet Explorer**, click **View**, click **Toolbars**, and click **Customize.** Then select **Show text labels** from the drop-down menu that appears on the lower right, across from **Text options.**

**In Windows Me, suddenly a CD won't start automatically when I insert it.**

1. Click **Start**, click **Settings**, click **Control Panel**, and then double-click the **System** icon.

2. Click the tab labeled Device Manager, click the '+' symbol next to **CDROM** and then double-click the entry for your CD-ROM drive.

3. Click the **Settings** tab, and make sure there is a check in the box next to **Auto Insert Notification.**

4. Click **OK**, click **Close**, and then click **Yes** when you are prompted to restart your computer.

If this does not fix the problem, see this Microsoft Knowledge Base article for an alternate solution: http://support.microsoft.com/?kbid=177880.

**When I reboot Windows Me, sometimes I see the message, "Windows could not upgrade the file %1 from %2 %1:%2."**

You have disabled System Restore and you have deleted the **_Restore** directory. As a result, Windows cannot find the directory necessary to create a restore point. Enable System Restore to fix this problem. (See Chapter 12 of this book for details on using System Restore.)

**How can I set Windows Explorer to always start at the root (beginning) of the C: drive, rather than in My Documents?**

See this Microsoft Knowledge Base article at http://support.microsoft.com/?kbid=130510.

**My Start button is blank (it no longer displays the word "Start"), and all the tabs in all windows are blank as well, with no text in them.**

This occurs when the text color chosen is the same as the background color. Click **Start**, click **Settings**, and click **Control Panel**. Double-click the **Display** icon, click the **Appearance** tab, and choose the Windows default scheme.

**My password is not being saved and/or the login screen keeps coming up when Windows 98/Me starts.**

There are numerous settings that need to be set correctly, so we will work through each one to ensure it is properly set.

1.  Click **Start**, click **Settings**, click **Control Panel**, and double-click the icon labeled **Passwords**. Click the tab titled **User Profiles** and make sure the option **All users of this computer use the same preferences and desktop settings** is selected. Then click **OK**.

2.  While in the Control Panel, see if you have an icon labeled **Tweak UI**. If so, double-click it, find the tab that says **Paranoia**, and make sure the option **Clear Last User at logon** is *not* checked. Click **OK**.

3.  Back in the Control Panel, double-click the icon labeled **Network** and make sure you have **Client for Microsoft Networks** as the first item listed. If **Microsoft Family Logon** or **Client for NetWare Networks** is listed (or both), click on them once and then click the **Remove** button.

4.  Under **Primary Network Logon**, select **Windows Logon**.

5.  Double-click **Client for Microsoft Networks** and ensure **Log on to Windows NT domain** is *not* checked. While in that window, ensure that **Quick logon** is selected, and then click **OK**.

6.  Click the **Access Control** tab at the top of the window and make sure the option **Share-level access control** is selected. Then click **OK**.

7. If you are asked to reboot, click **No**.

8. Close the Control Panel.

9. Click **Start**, click **Programs**, click **Accessories**, click **Communications**, and click **Dial-up Networking**. You should see the icon used to dial your ISP here. Right-click it and select **Properties**.

10. Click the **Networking** tab at the top of the window.

11. The *only* item that should be selected is **Enable software compression**. Make sure that **Log on to network** (if available) and all of the other options are not enabled. Below that, it says **Allowed network protocols**. Ensure that the last option, **TCP/IP**, is the *only* item selected. Then click **OK**.

12. Close any open windows.

13. Click **Start**, click **Run**, type **command**, and click **OK**.

14. Type **CD \Windows**, and press the ENTER key on your keyboard.

15. Type **del *.pwl** and press the ENTER key on your keyboard.

16. Type **exit** and press the ENTER key on your keyboard.

17. Click **Start**, click **Run**, type **regedit**, and click **OK**.

18. Click the + symbol next to **HKEY_LOCAL_MACHINE**.

19. Click the + symbol next to **Software**.

20. Click the + symbol next to **Microsoft**.

21. Click the + symbol next to **Windows**.

22. Click the + symbol next to **CurrentVersion**.

23. Click the + symbol next to **Network**.

24. Click the yellow folder next to **Real Mode Net**.

25. If you see a value named **AutoLogon**, click it and press the DELETE key on your keyboard. Once you have deleted it, close the window. (For more details on the AutoLogon procedure, visit www.wown.com/j_helmig/nologon .htm#AutoLogon.)

26. Click **Start**, click **Shutdown**, and choose **Restart**.

**27.** When Windows comes back up, a login screen should be displayed. For the name, type any name you like. Do not enter any text into the password line. Press the ENTER key on your keyboard.

**28.** If Windows asks for password verification, press the ENTER key again.

That's it—you're finished! The next time you restart Windows, the logon screen should not come up, and when you dial your ISP, the option to save your password should be enabled.

# Appendix E

## Windows XP Help!

This appendix contains a brief compilation of the most common Windows XP (Home and Professional Editions) problems and their possible solutions.

**Is there any way to force Outlook Express to minimize to the system tray?**

Sure, just download and install this free utility atwww.r2.com.au/downloads/index.html?id=hideoe.

**I cannot open attachments in Outlook Express 6.**

In Outlook Express, click **Tools**, click **Options**, and then click the **Security** tab. Make sure **Internet zone** is selected. Also, make sure the option **Do not allow attachments to be saved or opened that could potentially be a virus** is unchecked. Click **Apply**, and then click **OK**.

**When I click icons in the Control Panel, nothing happens, and when I press CTRL-ALT-DEL, I get an error message.**

Click **Start**, click **Run**, type **sfc /scannow**, and press ENTER. Once this completes, reboot the computer. If sfc (sfc is short for system file checker) discovers that a protected file has been overwritten, it retrieves the correct version. Note that you may be prompted for the Windows XP or Windows XP Service Pack 1 installation media during this process. More information can be found at http://support.microsoft.com/?kbid=318378.

**When I start Windows Update from Start menu, it says, "Windows Update was disabled by your system administrator."**

Click **Start**, click **Run**, type **gpedit.msc**, and press ENTER. Double-click **User Configuration**, double-click **Administrative Templates**, double-click **Windows Components**, and then double-click **Windows Update**. In the pane on the right, make sure the **remove access to Windows Update** policy is set to **Disabled** or **Not configured**.

**How can I get rid of the annoying Microsoft Messenger icon?**

To disable or completely remove Windows Messenger, Microsoft MVP Doug Knox created a small program you can download that will take care of this for you with a simple click of the mouse. You can learn more about this program and download it for free from www.dougknox.com/xp/utils/xp_mess_disable.htm.

**I somehow lost the Welcome screen, and now my computer comes up in classic logon.**

In the **Control Panel**, select **User Accounts**. Then click **Change the way users log on or off** and place a check in the box next to **Use the Welcome screen**. Finally, click the **Apply Options** button and close the remaining window.

**How can I disable "Out of hard drive space" error messages?**

See this Microsoft Knowledge Base article at http://support.microsoft.com/?kbid=285107.

**In Windows Explorer, how can I stop the confirmations for file deletions?**

Are you sure you want to do this? Just kidding! Right-click the **Recycle Bin** and select **Properties**. Uncheck **Display delete confirmation**.

**Whenever I select Open from the File menu to open a file (say, in Word or Internet Explorer), all my files in any directory or folder are shown in wrong alphabetical order.**

See this Microsoft Knowledge Base article at http://support.microsoft.com/?kbid=233526.

**How do you turn on password caching (so the computer will automatically remember your passwords) in Windows XP?**

See this Microsoft Knowledge Base article at http://support.microsoft.com/?kbid=235864.

# Appendix F

# Useful and Safe Freeware

There are numerous free utilities on the Internet, called *freeware*, that can help you maintain your computer and make it easier to use. Table F-1 lists the utilities I find to be the most useful. Use these utilities at your own risk and enjoyment.

In addition to these utilities, you may find the following free services useful:

- For Internet speed tests, visit www.dslreports.com or www.speedguide.net. You can use these web sites to determine how fast your Internet connection really is.

- Epinions, at www.epinions.com, is a web site you can use to share information about your experiences with any product and read about the experiences of other people.

| Utility | Description | Available From |
|---|---|---|
| WinZip | A great tool for compressing and uncompressing files | www.winzip.com |
| Magical Jelly Bean Keyfinder | A utility to determine what serial number was used to install Windows | www.magicaljellybean.com/keyfinder.shtml |
| EndItAll | A utility to close down all running programs; useful for Windows 95/98/Me users when attempting to use Scandisk or defragment the hard disk | www.pcmag.com/article2/0,4149,697,00.asp |
| RegClean | A utility designed by Microsoft to safely clean a Windows 95/98/Me Registry | www.winguides.com/software/display.php/23 |
| AVG Anti-Virus | A free antivirus program | www.grisoft.com |
| Zone Alarm | A free firewall | www.zonelabs.com |
| WinAmp | A great music player that doesn't use as many system resources as Windows Media Player | www.winamp.com |
| AdAware | A program designed to locate and remove spyware from your computer | www.lavasoftusa.com |
| SpyBot Search & Destroy | Another program designed to search for and destroy spyware on your computer | http://security.kolla.de |
| BootVis | A utility from Microsoft designed to speed up the boot process of Windows XP | www.microsoft.com/whdc/hwdev/platform/performance/fastboot/bootvis.mspx |
| MyFonts Font Manager | A Windows font-management utility | www.mytools.com |

**TABLE F-1**    Free Utilities on the Internet

| Utility | Description | Available From |
|---|---|---|
| Tweak UI | Utility for customizing Windows (For Windows 98/Me) | http://www.microsoft.com/ntworkstation/downloads/powertoys/networking/nttweakui.asp |
| Microsoft Power Toys for Windows XP | Utility for customizing Windows XP and adding additional features | http://www.microsoft.com/windowsxp/pro/downloads/powertoys.asp |
| Tiny Firewall | Another free firewall | www.tinysoftware.com |
| Windows XP Security Utilities | Steve Gibson's great free utility software to help secure your PC | http://grc.com/freepopular.htm |
| IE Maximizer | A program to ensure that your Internet Explorer and Outlook Express always open in a full screen | http://www.jiisoft.com/iemaximizer |

**TABLE F-1**    Free Utilities on the Internet *(continued)*

■   For recommendations of other useful freeware and shareware available on the Internet, sign up for PC World's free Daily Downloads newsletter at http://www.pcworld.com/resource/newsletters.

NOTE

*Other newsletters from product reviews to up-to-the-minute PC industry news can be selected here as well and you can unsubscribe from any of them at any time with ease.*

# Index

# INTERNATIONAL CONTACT INFORMATION

**AUSTRALIA**
McGraw-Hill Book Company
Australia Pty. Ltd.
TEL +61-2-9900-1800
FAX +61-2-9878-8881
http://www.mcgraw-hill.com.au
books-it_sydney@mcgraw-hill.com

**CANADA**
McGraw-Hill Ryerson Ltd.
TEL +905-430-5000
FAX +905-430-5020
http://www.mcgraw-hill.ca

**GREECE, MIDDLE EAST, & AFRICA
(Excluding South Africa)**
McGraw-Hill Hellas
TEL +30-210-6560-990
TEL +30-210-6560-993
TEL +30-210-6560-994
FAX +30-210-6545-525

**MEXICO (Also serving Latin America)**
McGraw-Hill Interamericana Editores
S.A. de C.V.
TEL +525-1500-5108
FAX +525-117-1589
http://www.mcgraw-hill.com.mx
carlos_ruiz@mcgraw-hill.com

**SINGAPORE (Serving Asia)**
McGraw-Hill Book Company
TEL +65-6863-1580
FAX +65-6862-3354
http://www.mcgraw-hill.com.sg
mghasia@mcgraw-hill.com

**SOUTH AFRICA**
McGraw-Hill South Africa
TEL +27-11-622-7512
FAX +27-11-622-9045
robyn_swanepoel@mcgraw-hill.com

**SPAIN**
McGraw-Hill/
Interamericana de España, S.A.U.
TEL +34-91-180-3000
FAX +34-91-372-8513
http://www.mcgraw-hill.es
professional@mcgraw-hill.es

**UNITED KINGDOM, NORTHERN,
EASTERN, & CENTRAL EUROPE**
McGraw-Hill Education Europe
TEL +44-1-628-502500
FAX +44-1-628-770224
http://www.mcgraw-hill.co.uk
emea_queries@mcgraw-hill.com

**ALL OTHER INQUIRIES Contact:**
McGraw-Hill/Osborne
TEL +1-510-420-7700
FAX +1-510-420-7703
http://www.osborne.com
omg_international@mcgraw-hill.com

# Sound Off!

Visit us at **www.osborne.com/bookregistration** and let us know what you thought of this book. While you're online you'll have the opportunity to register for newsletters and special offers from McGraw-Hill/Osborne.

## *We want to hear from you!*

# Sneak Peek

Visit us today at **www.betabooks.com** and see what's coming from McGraw-Hill/Osborne tomorrow!

Based on the successful software paradigm, Bet@Books™ allows computing professionals to view partial and sometimes complete text versions of selected titles online. Bet@Books™ viewing is free, invites comments and feedback, and allows you to "test drive" books in progress on the subjects that interest you the most.

Mc